Internet Your Way to a New Job (Third Edition)

How to *Really* Find a Job Online

By Alison Doyle

20660 Stevens Creek Blvd., Suite 210
Cupertino, CA 95014

Published by Happy About®
20660 Stevens Creek Blvd., Suite 210, Cupertino, CA 95014
http://happyabout.com

Third Printing: May 2011
Second Printing: May 2009
First Printing: March 2008
Paperback ISBN: 978-1-60005-199-9 (1-60005-199-5)
eBook ISBN: 978-1-60005-200-2 (1-60005-200-2)
Place of Publication: Silicon Valley, California, USA
Paperback Library of Congress Number: 2011926362

Trademarks

Warning and Disclaimer

Acknowledgments

Thank you, most of all, to my husband, Michael, and my daughter, Katie, for their support while I wrote this book. I appreciate your advice, patience, and your manuscript reading skills. Without you both, I couldn't do what I do.

I also appreciate the rest of my family, the career and job search experts who shared their expertise, and the job seekers who took the time to write to me. You have all provided me with insight, commentary, and advice that helped make this book possible.

Thanks to you all.

Alison Doyle

A Message from Happy About®

Thank you for your purchase of this Happy About book. It is available online at http://happyabout.com/InternetYourWaytoaNewJob.php or at other online and physical bookstores.

- Please contact us for quantity discounts at sales@happyabout.info
- If you want to be informed by email of upcoming Happy About® books, please email bookupdate@happyabout.info

Happy About is interested in you if you are an author who would like to submit a non-fiction book proposal or a corporation that would like to have a book written for you. Please contact us by email editorial@happyabout.info or phone (1-408-257-3000).

Other Happy About books available include:

- I'm at a Networking Event—Now What???:
  http://happyabout.com/networking-event.php
- Storytelling About Your Brand Online & Offline:
  http://happyabout.com/storytelling.php
- I'm on LinkedIn—Now What???:
  http://happyabout.com/linkedinhelp.php
- Happy About My Resume:
  http://happyabout.com/myresume.php
- Happy About The Career Alphabet:
  http://happyabout.com/happyaboutcareeralphabet.php
- Fast Track Guide to a Professional Job Search:
  http://happyabout.com/fasttrackjobsearch.php
- The Successful Introvert:
  http://happyabout.com/thesuccessfulintrovert.php
- #ENTRYLEVELtweet Book01:
  http://happyabout.com/thinkaha/entryleveltweet01.php
- #JOBSEARCHtweet Book01:
  http://happyabout.com/thinkaha/jobsearchtweet01.php
- #MILLENNIALtweet Book01:
  http://happyabout.com/thinkaha/millennialtweet01.php
- Rule #1: Stop Talking!:
  http://happyabout.com/listenerspress/stoptalking.php
- Blitz the Ladder:
  http://happyabout.com/blitz.php
- 42 Rules of Cold Calling Executives:
  http://happyabout.com/42rules/coldcallingexecutives.php
- 42 Rules to Jumpstart Your Professional Success:
  http://happyabout.com/42rules/jumpstartprofessionalservices.php

Contents

Introduction 1

Chapter 1 **Building Your Professional Brand** **3**

What's Your Brand? 4
How to Create Your Professional Brand. 6
LinkedIn for Professional Networking. 6
VisualCV—Your Online Resume 7
Facebook for Personal and
Professional Networking. 9
Twitter. 9
More Networking Sites 11
Which Sites to Use 12
What to Include in Your Profile. 12
Professional and Personal Networking. 14
Connect Your Networks 15
Writing a Blog. 15
Personal Websites 17
Optimize Yourself. 17
Why Search Engine Optimization
(SEO) Is Important 18
More on Professional Branding 19

Chapter 2 **Online Career Networking** **21**

Benefits of Networking 21
Networking—Then vs. Now 22
Who to Include in Your Network. 23
How to Use Your Network 24
How to Connect 24
Connect with Relevant Contacts 24
Using Your Connections in Your Job Search 25
Searching for Jobs on LinkedIn 26
Getting Found on LinkedIn. 28
Staying in Touch. 28
Strategies to Build Your Network 29
Work Your Connections 29
Top Networking Sites 30
Choose Your Networks. 34

Chapter 3 | **Resumes and Cover Letters** **35**

Creating a Resume 35
The Details Matter 38
The Truth Matters. 38
Age-Proof Your Resume 39
Targeted Resumes. 40
Resume Reviews. 40
The Resume Black Hole 40
Writing Cover Letters 41
Review Sample Cover Letters 43
Sending Your Resume and Letters 45
What (and What Not) to Do 46
Saying Thank You 47

Chapter 4 | **How to Job Search Online** **49**

How to Start a Job Search 49
Job Search Plan. 51
Email Accounts 51
Store Your Documents. 51
A Place to Work 52
Job Search Tools 53
Get Organized 54
Review Job Options 54
Get Help. 55
Be Active 56
How to Apply for Jobs Online. 57
How to Follow Up. 58
Follow-Up Timing 59
When You Don't Hear Back 60
Don't Stop and Don't Wait 60

Chapter 5 | **Where to Find Jobs** **63**

Company Websites 65
Company Research Sites 65
Job Search Sites 66
Top Job Banks. 67
Job Search Engines. 68
Top Job Search Engines 69
Niche Job Search Engines. 69
Local Job Search 70
Networking Sites 70
Niche Sites. 71

Social Networking Sites 72
College Job Sites 73
Job Searching Tips. 74
Keep Track 75

Chapter 6 | **Social Recruiting 77**

Social Recruiting Overview. 77
Talent Networks 78
Candidate Sourcing 79
Social Recruiting and Your Career. 80

Chapter 7 | **Active vs. Passive Job Seeking 83**

Passive and Active Job Seeking Overview 83
How Hiring Managers and Recruiters
Seek Passive Candidates. 84
Use Passive Job Seeking to Your Advantage 86
How to Ensure Employers Find You. 89
How to Get Jobs to Come to You. 89
Build Bridges, Don't Burn Them 91

Chapter 8 | **Online Job Search Management Tools . . . 93**

JibberJobber. 94
Online Job Search Management 95
Email Options 95
Calendars 96
Documents 98
More Tools 99

Chapter 9 | **Online Communications 101**

The Simple Solution 101
Email. 103
Instant Message (IM) 104
Networking Site Messaging 105
Video Resumes, Profiles, and Interviewing 105
Video Interview Tips. 107
The Benefits of Effective Communication. 108

Chapter 10 | **Job Search Apps 111**

Job Search Apps Overview 111
iPhone and iPad Apps .112
Facebook Apps. 113

Chapter 11 | **Privacy and Safety Issues** 115

How to Not Find a Job Online 115
Protect Your Privacy 115
What Employers Can Find Out About You.......117
Privacy Concerns.........................118
Social Networking Privacy Settings 120
How to Avoid Scams 120
Confidential Job Searching 122

Chapter 12 | **Job Search Tips from the Experts** 125

Appendix A | **Top Job and Networking Websites** 133

Author | About the Author 137

Books | Other Happy About® Books.................139

Introduction

Just a few years ago, you could upload your resume to one of the top job sites and, with a few mouse clicks, consider your job search well under way. Today, that isn't enough. The job market is becoming increasingly competitive. Hiring managers are overwhelmed with applications and are looking at new and different ways to recruit online.

Hiring has changed and so has job searching. It's more complex than it used to be. Gone are the days when you could just send a resume and wait for a phone call to set up an interview. Now, job seekers need to be prepared to use all the online job search tools to their advantage.

This means that you need to do more than just posting your resume on Monster, CareerBuilder, or Dice, though they still can be an effective part of your job search. In addition to job searching the traditional way, you need to be actively networking online and taking advantage of the ways social media sites can enhance your job search.

It can be complicated and confusing. Career expert and author of *The Job Search Solution*, Tony Beshara, says, "Most job seekers don't realize how difficult this market is. They need massive numbers of contacts, cold calls, interviews, and follow up interviews to get a job. It is going to take a while and they can't get discouraged. They have to work a "system" of getting a job, i.e., a tremendous number of activities that lead to interviews, performing well on those interviews, and negotiating a job offer. Getting a new job is a job in itself!"

Anyone, and that's almost everyone at some point in their career, seeking a job or career change should be aware of what tools and techniques are available, and how you can utilize them to expedite your job search—and get that new job. That includes building a professional brand to promote yourself, using job sites, social and career networking sites, blogs, instant messaging, as well as the tools that can help you manage and expedite your job search and build your career.

Job searching has changed from a once or twice in a lifetime endeavor into what is, for some people, a career-long process of networking with contacts, changing jobs or careers, and moving up (or even choosing to move down) the career ladder.

This book will provide what you need to know and step you through the process of online job searching, professional branding, social and professional networking, and career building with uncomplicated advice, tips, and techniques on how to effectively find a new job.

Online job searching often seems like it can be a complicated endeavor. It doesn't have to be. There are numerous tips you can use to make the process smooth and simple. In fact, there are lots of people who have found a new job without even leaving their house, including applying, interviewing, and getting hired.

You can be successful with your online job search as well. I'll provide you with everything you need to know on how to build your career and find a new job.

1 Building Your Professional Brand

You might think that I'm giving you backwards advice, but I'm not. Before you start writing or updating your resume or applying for a job, you need to start building your online presence. The only exception would be if you're looking for a retail, seasonal, temporary, or similar job, where the hiring considerations are different and it's easier to apply and to get hired. In that case, it certainly doesn't hurt to have a professional presence online, but it's not a necessity.

It's important to build your brand in order to:

1. **Create** a professional presence on the Internet.
2. **Market** yourself as a strong candidate for employers.
3. **Connect** with contacts who will help you with your job search.
4. **Help** prospective employers find you.

What's Your Brand?

In a nutshell, your brand is your online presence. You can, and should, have your own brand, just like Tiffany's has for fine jewelry or Subway has for submarine sandwiches.

Your professional brand needs to reflect your skills, your interests, and your expertise. So, when someone finds information about you online, it connects them to who you are and what you can do.

Like it or not, if an employer is considering you for a job, they are going to Google you to see what they can find. You don't want prospective employers looking at pictures of your summer vacation or a party where you might have overindulged a little. The rule of thumb I always use is the "grandma" standard. If there is something that you wouldn't want your grandmother (or your mom) to see on the web, you don't want a prospective employer to view it either.

I still cringe at the photos I've seen on some Facebook pages and in blogs. Some of the descriptions of the good times had by all are cringe-worthy, too, when you look at them from a "what they can do to your job search" perspective.

Remember, once you put something online (or your friends do) it's there just about forever. Perhaps employers shouldn't consider your personal life as relevant to your qualifications for a job, but they do. That's why you need to make your brand one that's going to impress both potential employers and your networking contacts (the people who will help you find a job).

Here's an example of a good professional presence, if I do say so myself. Google "Alison Doyle" and take a look at the search results. You won't find anything regarding my summer vacation or my personal life. Instead, you'll find:

- my About.com Job Searching site (http://jobsearch.about.com)

- my bio (http://jobsearch.about.com/mbiopage.htm)

- my LinkedIn Profile (http://linkedin.com/in/alisondoyle)

- the About.com Job Search LinkedIn Group
  (http://www.linkedin.com/groups?home=&gid=98687)

- my VisualCV (http://www.visualcv.com/alisondoyle)

- my blog (http://alisondoyle.typepad.com)

- my Facebook page (http://tinyurl.com/47kn5a7)
  [facebook.com/people/Alison-Doyle/12203480]

- the About.com Job Search Facebook page
  (http://www.facebook.com/aboutjobsearch)

- my website (http://alisondoyle.com)

- my book listings on Amazon

That's by design. It wasn't hard to do, and I'll show you how you can build a brand that you're comfortable sharing online.

Another good example of excellent brand building is what Jason Alba (http://jasonalba.com), CEO of JibberJobber.com and author of *I'm on LinkedIn—Now What???* has achieved. Google "Jason Alba" and you'll see that all the results are related to his career: JibberJobber, his blog, his website, and his LinkedIn profile.

When you look at the search results for both Jason and me, you'll see that we're experts on job searching, careers, and job search management. That's what we do, and it's immediately apparent what our area of expertise is.

Try the same searches with Yahoo! and you'll get similar results. It's a little harder if you have a last name that lots of other people share, but even if you don't get into the top ten rankings for your name, your goal is to get top results to include all "good" content and none of the things you don't want grandma to see.

How to Create Your Professional Brand

The first step in creating your professional brand is to consider what you want to highlight. For example, if you're a computer programmer, you'll want to highlight your technical skills. If you're a marketing professional, you'll want to promote your public relations/marketing experience. When you have multiple areas of expertise, it's best to choose one to focus on. A diluted brand isn't going to be as helpful as one that captures your experience clearly.

William Arruda, founder of Reach, the global leader of personal branding, author of *Career Distinction* and curator at personalbranding.tv explains, "An important element of your brand is differentiation. To determine your differentiation, think about what you have in common with others who are seeking the same position. Then, think about what makes you stand out—what unique value you have to offer. Once you know that, you can modify your career marketing tools to reflect that unique value. This is the key to effective personal branding."

As I mentioned, when you search for me online you'll find me as soon as you Google my name, and you will know right away that I write about careers and job searching. That's the point you want to get to with your professional brand.

Once you have decided on a focus, create a profile on at least some of the top networking sites. That's the first step in building your own brand.

LinkedIn for Professional Networking

LinkedIn is the professional place to be. I don't know anyone who is in any type of professional position who doesn't have a LinkedIn profile. The first step is to join LinkedIn (http://www.linkedin.com), and then you can create your profile.

Make your profile as detailed as possible. The more information you provide, the more there will be for recruiters and networking contacts to read about you. Use the professional Summary section of your profile to showcase your expertise. You can use the headline for a quick description (mine says Job Search Expert and Writer) and the summary to list your experience and goals. Select your industry of expertise as well.

Contact Settings are important. That's how employers, recruiters, and connections will identify what you want to be contacted about and what you are interested in. Contact Setting options include:

- career opportunities

- consulting offers

- new ventures

- job inquiries

- reference requests

Don't forget to include links to your website, blog, etc., if you have them, in the Additional Information section of your profile. They will help you send contacts to sites that contain even more information about you.

Also, use your LinkedIn profile as a personal branding tool. Jason Alba suggests, "Put your LinkedIn URL in your email signature and when you comment on blogs and forums. This makes it easy for people to learn more about you. You never know who will see your profile, considering how easy it is to forward an email to friends and contacts."

VisualCV—Your Online Resume

A VisualCV (http://visualcv.com) is an online resume that includes all the facets of a traditional resume and then some. There are add-ons like video, images, and links to projects, websites, and accomplishments to help you make a dynamic, professional presentation to your connections, to hiring managers, and to recruiters. A VisualCV is not only professional; it's quick and easy to create. You can copy and paste from your original resume or start from scratch with VisualCV's Resume Builder.

Users can print a PDF version of their VisualCV, share updates on LinkedIn, Facebook, Twitter, and other social media sites, and use the LinkedIn Connector to quickly send their VisualCV URL to their LinkedIn profile.

In addition, there are hundreds of companies and recruiters signed up at VisualCV.com to find and attract professional candidates. So, creating a VisualCV is another way to get noticed by employers.

Phillip Merrick, VisualCV's cofounder explains how VisualCV can help your job search:

> VisualCV is an essential tool for today's job seeker. With a VisualCV you can build and manage a more engaging Internet-based resume (for free) that helps you show and tell your professional experience. You can combine work samples, references, audio, video and more—all on a single trackable web page. Plus, VisualCV is easy to use and you're in control of your privacy. Your VisualCV is designed to go viral if you choose; you can share your VisualCV via your unique URL, LinkedIn, Facebook, Twitter, and more.
>
> Companies have joined VisualCV to find and attract professionals for their open positions. They are finding that they can evaluate a professional faster when they have a VisualCV instead of a traditional resume. The ultimate goal is to help connect companies and professionals in a faster, more efficient manner. We have hundreds of companies signed up to receive VisualCVs from professionals.
>
> VisualCV is fast becoming the career cornerstone of an individual's personal brand online that is useful beyond active job search. Fully portable, a VisualCV can be used anywhere you have a digital presence in the same way as a business card or bio, to help enrich business networking opportunities.

Facebook for Personal and Professional Networking

There used to be a school of thought that said Facebook is for kids. It's not anymore. Facebook's demographics include all age groups. To say that almost everyone is using it wouldn't be an exaggeration. In addition, Facebook is increasingly being used for professional networking, as well as for personal networking. Companies are using Facebook to recruit, and job seekers are increasingly tapping Facebook to help with their job search.

Sign up on Facebook (http://facebook.com), and then you will be able to create a profile. Facebook has more bells and whistles (photos, music, lots of gadgets and widgets) than LinkedIn, but you don't need to use them. If you're using Facebook for professional networking and building your brand, keep it as simple as possible.

Keep in mind that the lines between personal and professional networking have blurred, especially for Generation Y users. Facebook has evolved as its original users have grown up and entered the workplace. For many of those users, there aren't as many boundaries between work and play as there are for those of us who are a bit older. Your Facebook Friends can connect you with jobs and vice versa, as well as providing opportunities for socializing.

It is important to be really careful about your privacy settings. Decide who you want to see what and restrict your personal information, including photos and possibly your wall, to your Friends.

Twitter

It seems like everyone is talking about Twitter (http://twitter.com). Twitter is a social networking and microblogging service. Individuals use Twitter to stay in touch and to make new connections. Companies and job boards post job openings on Twitter, and job seekers network through Twitter to help facilitate their job search.

Users post updates (tweets) on Twitter that are displayed on their profile page and delivered to other users who have signed up to receive them. The catch is that your posts can't be any longer than 140 characters, so you need to be concise.

Each user has a name that you can use to send messages, and a dedicated URL. Mine is http://twitter.com/AlisonDoyle and you can connect with me on Twitter @AlisonDoyle.

There are jobs posted directly on Twitter. On sites like JobShouts (@jobshouts), employers can post jobs for free. Those jobs are then automatically "tweeted" to users on Twitter. Twit Job Search, another Twitter based job site (@twitjobsearch), allows users to search Twitter for job postings by keyword and location. You can search Twitter for jobs using the web as well. Visit twitjobsearch.com (http://twitjobsearch.com) to search for job postings.

Robin Eads, cofounder of JobShouts.com, shares the concept behind JobShouts: "So what if there was a way to reach millions of people with a job ad that cost nothing to the employer? We decided that this concept would offer value to recruiters everywhere, whether corporate or agency. By integrating a job board with Twitter (and eventually other social media platforms such as Facebook), we are helping employers and job seekers connect through a social media channel they may already be using. JobShouts was founded with the purpose of reaching a virtually untapped audience of job seekers and employers. Since JobShouts doesn't allow spam, MLM or work-at-home jobs, job seekers can be confident that the job leads they are receiving are legitimate."

TweetMyJobs.com (http://tweetmyjobs.com) (@tweetmyjobs) is the largest Twitter job board. It includes almost 10,000 vertical job channels segmented by geography, job type, and industry. Job seekers can receive notifications of new jobs via their Twitter feed or their cell phone.

For those in need of job search assistance, JobAngels (@jobangels) is a wonderful Twitter resource. JobAngels began as "just" an idea. It started with one tweet, with the objective of asking those who could to help one person find a job. It's grown tremendously since then. Job seekers are posting the types of positions they are looking for and getting job leads and assistance with their job search. Offers of help keep pouring in—job postings, offers to help with resumes, job search advice, networking contacts, and more.

Kristen Fischer, author of *Ramen Noodles, Rent and Resumes: An After-College Guide to Life* (http://ramenrentresumes.com) has good advice for finding job sites and career experts to follow on Twitter:

> Use the Twitter search tool and search words like "career" or "jobs" to find career experts and existing job boards. You'll get original information from the career experts who frequently tweet with links to resources and articles that can help improve your job hunt strategies.
>
> Another technique you may want to try is using LinkedIn to search for career experts, job hunting professionals and other job search resources. Once you get the names of people you want to follow, use the Twitter search tool to search for his or her name, specifically. Twitter's search tool isn't all-encompassing; so I like to use LinkedIn to look at people I want to add and then find them on Twitter. I think you can get a lot more information on LinkedIn. And those on LinkedIn grasp technology; so they're likely on Twitter, too.

More Networking Sites

There are many more networking sites that you can use. You'll find a directory on my About.com Job Search site (http://tinyurl.com/24ld2h) [jobsearch.about.com/od/networkingsites/Career_and_Social_Networking_Sites.htm]. Some are niche sites focused on a specific audience. For example, 85 Broads is for women from partner colleges. You'll need an email address from your school to sign up. If you are a graduate, check with your alumni office. They may be able to provide you with an email address to use when you register.

Ning is a website where users can create, customize, and share a social network. Networkers have used Ning to create online social networks about many topics, including job searching. Some of the employment-related social networks are based on industry or location while others, such as Secrets of the Job Hunt Network, at http://www.secretsofthejobhunt.com, are broader.

Which Sites to Use

Do you need to create a profile on every networking site there is? I don't think so. First of all, there are more sites than you can easily keep track of. It's also better to have a few good profiles that you can keep updated without spending all day working on online networking, which you could easily do.

I recommend starting with LinkedIn, VisualCV, and Facebook. Once you have created detailed profiles on those sites, you can consider adding profiles at other sites, but don't overdo it.

What to Include in Your Profile

Keep your profiles simple. Remember that we're discussing professional networking, so avoid adding Facebook applications that don't relate to your job search. Prospective employers won't want to get gifts or candy from you, see who you think is hot or not, hug you, or do most of the thousands of other applications you can add to your profile.

Include the following in your profile:

- Education

- Work experience (current and past)

- Summary of your background (LinkedIn)

- Industry (LinkedIn)

- Location

- Websites

- Email address (you may not want to make it public)

In addition to bolstering your professional presence, fully completing your profile will allow contacts to search the networking sites and find you. That's especially helpful when you want to be found by recruiters or hiring managers looking for someone with your skills and experience.

Add Your Photo

All the top networking sites allow you to add a photo. If you use the same photo on all the sites, it will help build your brand—viewers will immediately recognize you wherever they come across you on the web.

The photo you are going to upload doesn't need to be professionally taken, but you need to look professional. It should be a head/shoulders shot and you should wear appropriate business attire. I've had good luck taking photos at home with a digital camera.

You can easily upload a photo by following the directions on the site. Basically, you'll click and find the photo on the hard drive of your computer, and the system will upload it. There may be image uploading size and quality restrictions, so check the guidelines before you upload the picture.

Expand Your Profile

Now that you have created a basic profile or two, you'll want to expand it. My profile (http://linkedin.com/in/alisondoyle) includes recommendations from clients and colleagues. I would also include recommendations from coworkers and customers. Positive recommendations will impress those who read your profile.

A good way to get recommendations is to give them. Write a few recommendations for contacts you know and then ask them if they would mind reciprocating. You've helped someone else, so they may be more likely to help you in return.

Keep Track

Create a list of the sites (and add them to your Favorites in your browser) where you have created profiles, so you can get to them easily. Or, set up a Google or Yahoo! home page and add links or bookmarks to your page, so you can easily get to your profiles.

Keep track of your login information and your passwords. I have a Passwords folder in my Outlook Email and I email myself a message that includes the link to my login, my login email address or name, and my password. That way I don't have to remember multiple logins.

Another option is to keep a spreadsheet with the same information. That way you can readily locate it if you need it. You can set up an Excel table with a list of URLs, passwords, and login information.

There are also sites like RoboForm and Password Safe that will keep track of your passwords for you. That's another option for keeping track of your login information.

Professional and Personal Networking

I'll go into more detail on how to network in Chapter 2, but you will want to get started building your network now, before you actually start your job search. That way, you'll have some of the stepping stones in place to get your job search moving along at a quick pace.

Visit the sites where you have created profiles. Look for people you know. You can find colleagues, classmates, even contacts from your web mail accounts (Gmail, Yahoo!, AOL) and from your Outlook contacts on LinkedIn. Facebook allows you to invite your friends from your Yahoo!, Hotmail, AOL, Gmail, or MSN address book. On both sites, you can search for people you know. Invite your contacts to connect with you and you'll have the beginning of an online career network you can use to enhance your job search.

Keep in mind, as well, that most people change jobs ten to fifteen times during their career. So, even though this may sound like a lot of work, it's not a one-shot deal. You will be able to use your network right now and in the future, when you are ready to job search again.

Another benefit to having online networks is that you don't have to keep track of your contacts' changing email addresses. You'll be able to message them directly from the networking site you are using. It's an excellent way to stay in touch.

Connect Your Networks

It's easy to connect all your networks. Link to your VisualCV from your LinkedIn Profile and vice versa. If you're using Facebook for professional networking, include links to your other networking site profiles. Some sites have automated widgets that add links (you simply click to add your profile from a certain site). With others you can copy and paste the links into your profile.

Why does it matter? When a recruiter, for example, looks at your LinkedIn Profile and sees your VisualCV in the Additional Information section, he or she will then be able to click on the link to your VisualCV and view even more information that will enhance your value as a prospective candidate.

You don't know how or where a company or connection will find you, so cross-promoting your various profiles enables them to readily find all the information that's available online that showcases your skills, abilities, professional experience, and educational background.

Writing a Blog

A blog (web log) is another good way to build your brand and share your credentials with the world. You don't have to spend a lot of time or money on it. There are free blog platforms available; a blog is easy to set up, and you can use a template (no need to know web design) to create your blog.

Writing a blog can be fun, as well as career enhancing. If you pick a topic you're informed on, you can share your advice and experiences, and you'll have a resume-building asset to share with employers and contacts.

For example, if you're in the insurance business, consider writing a blog about insurance trends or tips for selecting and buying insurance. Or, if you're a riding instructor, blog about horse shows or give advice to riders or instructors. Choose a topic that matches your interests (so it's not boring to write) and your career goals.

Blog Platforms

- Blog.com

- Blogger.com

- Tumblr.com

- Typepad.com

- Wordpress.com

TIPS FOR CREATING YOUR BLOG

- Use your name as the Blog Title, if it's available.

- Choose a simple, easy-to-read template.

- Focus your blog. Even though the temptation can be to ramble on about everything and anything, your blog should be focused on your area of expertise.

- Include links to your online profiles.

- Update your blog regularly, even if it's only once a week. There's nothing worse than an "ancient" blog floating around in cyberspace.

Marketing Your Blog

From your blog, link to LinkedIn, Facebook, VisualCV, Twitter, and any other profiles you have. That way, if someone reads your blog, they can find out more about you on the other sites and vice versa.

List your blog on your resume. It will provide additional credentials of your expertise. When your blog adds value to your candidacy, mention it in your cover letters.

Personal Websites

It took me quite a bit of work to acquire the http://alisondoyle.com domain because someone had purchased it years ago, before I had a clue I might need a domain to market myself and my work. It might be easier for you, especially if you don't have a name that's similar to someone famous, like Stephen King or Oprah Winfrey.

If you can get your domain (http://www.yourname.com), go for it. It will be another way for you to build the brand that is you. Sites like Go Daddy make it quick and easy to get and set up domains, if the domain name is available. You can then create a personal website or forward your domain to your blog. The latter can be easier if you don't want to think about designing, maintaining, and editing a website.

Optimize Yourself

Now that you've spent some time building an online presence, there are just a few more steps to ensure all the time you spent was put to good use. It's very likely that employers are going to Google you (search Google to find out what they can about you) if they are considering you for employment.

Why Search Engine Optimization (SEO) Is Important

Search engine optimization is what websites do to get a high ranking in Google, Yahoo!, MSN, and the other search engines. A high ranking means that your site shows up in the first results for that search term. For example, if you sell gift baskets, you want to do your best to get your site high up in the search results when someone looks for the term *gift baskets*; that's because users are more likely to click on the highest results.

Your goal in optimizing yourself is to ensure that your profiles, your blog, and the rest of your online professional presence shows up high in the search results when a prospective employer searches for your name. Because you've taken the time to create impressive web content, you are better positioned to be an attractive candidate to these employers.

All that linking back and forth we just did (from your profiles to your blog and vice versa) is also part of optimizing. It wasn't just to get people from one site to the other, though that is important as well. The cross-linking shows the search engines that your name (the name of your profiles and your blog) has weight, and that helps it achieve a higher ranking.

TIPS FOR OPTIMIZING YOUR WEBSITE, PROFILES, AND BLOGS

- Set up a Vanity URL for your LinkedIn Profile (http://linkedin.com/yourname). You can customize the URL of your public profile on the Edit My Profile page.

- Promote your LinkedIn profile with a personalized "View My LinkedIn Profile" button linking to your profile.

- You can find the button under Edit Profile on LinkedIn.

- Add the button to your blog and to your website, if you have one.

- Use your name as often as possible: in titles, content, and links.

- Include your area of expertise as often as possible in your blog posts.

- If you have a personal website, make sure that you include links to your profiles and your blogs.

More on Professional Branding

Dan Schawbel's Personal Branding Blog
(http://www.personalbrandingblog.com) is full of advice on how you can build your brand. Dan's an expert. In fact, if you Google "Dan Schawbel" you will get thousands of results that include his name. You may not get that many results for yourself, but you should be able to get a decent amount.

Dan explains why branding is valuable: "Personal branding is about distinguishing yourself from other applicants applying for the same job. By developing a memorable brand both online and offline, you can extend your reach and visibility and have the opportunity to be recruited based on your skills, personality, appearance, and total value. As a brand, you are empowered to be your own manager, spokesperson, and most importantly yourself. Start a blog, join social networks and associations that represent the types of individuals you want to surround yourself with and, in the end, you will be compensated based on what you enjoy."

Do keep in mind that building your professional brand and rising in the search engine ranks can take time. Don't expect it to happen overnight. Keep working on it, even as your job search progresses. Continue after you have found your next job. Building your brand works in conjunction with building your career and should be a career-long endeavor. In fact, it can be a way to launch a career change in midlife or even later.

The stronger your brand, the more positive the impression you will make on those who find you online; connections who can help build your career, including colleagues, clients, and future employers. They will readily be able to identify you as an expert in your field, and can see your employment history, your backgrounds, your skills, and your experience at a glance.

RELATED RESOURCES

- 85 Broads (http://85broads.com)
- Facebook (http://facebook.com)
- Google (http://google.com)
- LinkedIn (http://linkedin.com)
- Twitter (http://www.twitter.com)
- VisualCV (http://visualcv.com)

2 | Online Career Networking

Benefits of Networking

Your job search/career network includes the people who can help you find a new job, get a promotion, change careers, get a client, give you a recommendation, or who are willing to assist you in any number of ways. In many cases, all you have to do is ask.

Your network should include colleagues, clients, friends, and just about anyone who might be able to assist you, either now or in the future.

Who you know can be as important as what you know. Sometimes, it can be even more important. On a very basic level, it can help you get a job. I got my first job at the local grocery store because my mom was a regular customer and she asked if they were hiring.

During all the years since I worked there, I've always stopped in to say hello whenever I was in the area. I still get a warm welcome and some of the employees are still working there. That's maintaining your network. Even though I probably won't need those former coworkers, it never hurts to stay in touch.

In another, professional-level example, when a company I worked for was going out of business, I was offered a job by a competitor who used to work for the company. We had stayed in touch after he had moved on to start his own business. I let him know I would be available, and I had an open job offer for whenever I wanted to come to work.

I didn't accept the job. At that point, I thought a career change, with less travel and fewer hours, was in order. However, I declined gracefully, and I've stayed in touch with my contact over the years. We still have lunch every once in a while, even though our careers don't have much of a connection any longer.

Besides helping you find jobs and get hired, your contacts can provide you with referrals and references. They can also help you discover information about prospective industries and employers. For example, many colleges have career networks (check with your alma mater if you're a college graduate) where alumni and students can contact alumni in industries, positions, companies, and locations of interest. What better way is there to get the inside scoop on jobs and careers that interest you?

Networking—Then vs. Now

Back when I first starting networking, building a network was more work. To be honest, I don't think I even thought of it as networking. It was keeping in touch with people I had enjoyed working with and with whom I didn't want to lose contact. There wasn't such a thing as online networking; you stayed in touch via phone calls, lunches, and then email. It's much easier now, of course, because you can do all that networking online. In fact, I have people in my network whom I haven't met in person and may never have an opportunity to meet.

The basic premise of networking hasn't changed. The goal remains to leverage people you know to help you find a job and to move up (or down) the career ladder. We just do it differently. It's much easier today. You can network, stay in touch, find inside information on companies, and get referrals from your home computer with a few clicks of your mouse.

Who to Include in Your Network

Who should you include in your network? You will want to include just about anyone and everyone you know, because you never know who will be able to help you.

My vet hired my niece for an office position, because we happened to be chatting about her needing an employee and my niece needing a job. A dental assistant at my dentist's office was looking for a part-time job at a riding stable, and I happened to know of an opening at a local farm. I was approached via LinkedIn (http://linkedin.com) by a former colleague who was hiring for a software designer position, and I happened to know the perfect person for him. He interviewed her and hired her on the spot.

Hiring managers like referrals, because it saves them from screening (sometimes hundreds) of resumes. When a candidate is referred by someone they know, they can get a good sense of the applicant's skills and a recommendation in advance of the screening process. It saves time and helps them build a stronger pool of candidates. That's why companies often pay hiring bonuses to employees who recommend candidates.

Your network should include:

- Business connections

- College alumni

- Company alumni (former coworkers and managers)

- Colleagues

- Clients

- Customers

- Family

- Friends and neighbors

How to Use Your Network

You've created a profile on a networking site, what next? The next step is to find contacts so you can add to your network. On most networking sites, you can search globally for past and present colleagues and classmates, and you can add contacts from your email accounts. There are also advanced search options you can use to find a specific individual, searching by name, keyword, location, group, etc.

How to Connect

Once you have found people to connect with, you need to invite them to connect with you. Facebook users can add the person as a friend and your connection will receive a message saying that they have been added to your contacts. They can accept or decline your invitation.

On LinkedIn, you can send an email message, send InMail, or ask for an introduction from a mutual connection. There's a standard system message inviting the person to connect, but you can customize it, which is always a good idea. If you're a member of a LinkedIn Group, you may be able to contact another group member directly to connect.

Connect with Relevant Contacts

What's important about connecting on any networking site is not to waste your time, or anyone else's, connecting with people who don't have a clue who you are. I turn down any requests for connections from people I don't know or who aren't recommended by someone I know. Why? Because, unless I can see that we have someone in common, there is no need for me to join their network or vice versa.

The key is to have "real" contacts, people who know you and are willing to help you, rather than hundreds of meaningless connections. So please don't invite everyone and anyone you ever heard of—you will annoy some of them, and the others aren't going to be much use to you if they can't recommend your work or candidacy for employment.

Think "relevancy" when you're making connections. How do I know the person and how might they be able to help me and how can I help them?

Using Your Connections in Your Job Search

Here's a good example of relevancy. Avram, while in the midst of a job change, used LinkedIn to contact people who worked at the companies he was interviewing with. He suggests, "Contact people who worked at the company before via LinkedIn and see if they'll give you the lowdown." He was able to find out good information about the organizations and the positions that he was interested in.

In some cases, the information you find out about the job and the company will help when it comes to interviewing; the information you gathered could be used for preparation. In other cases, it may help you decide that you don't want the job. That's fine, too. It's much better to turn down a job that isn't a good fit than it is to have to start your job search over because your new job didn't work out.

In another case, Sylvia posted her profile, made a lot of connections, and subsequently (and coincidentally) ended up being laid off. She let all her connections know she was looking for a new job and heard from an interested employer almost immediately.

A word of warning though—you need to be really careful who you tell that you are looking for work. I know someone who announced that she was looking for a new job. A connection forwarded the message to her boss and she ended up losing her job before she was prepared to go. Her boss was not amused at finding out thirdhand that she was planning on leaving the company.

Searching for Jobs on LinkedIn

As well as using your connections to help with your job search, you can look for jobs directly on LinkedIn. First, review LinkedIn's suggestions for finding jobs:

- Keep your profile updated and make sure it's complete.

- Get recommendations.

- Get connections—so you have contacts at as many companies as possible.

- Download the JobsInsider tool—it will show you how you are connected at jobs listed online (at sites like Monster, CareerBuilder, SimplyHired, Dice, and Craigslist) and you can request an introduction to the hiring manager.

There are jobs posted directly on LinkedIn by companies, as well as other jobs that SimplyHired, the job search engine, lists.

You can search for jobs by keyword, country, and postal code. If the job is listed directly on LinkedIn (rather than a general listing), you'll see how you're connected (1st, 2nd, 3rd, etc.) to the hiring manager and you can apply online and/or request a referral.

Here's an example: I clicked on a Content Manager position. It was listed directly on LinkedIn and nine of my connections either knew the hiring manager or could connect me with someone who did. If I was interested in applying, I could upload a cover letter and ask for a referral for the job.

The standard referral letter looks like this:

I have asked my connection John Doe to provide a short recommendation for my qualifications for the position you posted titled 'Content Management.' Here's a link to the job:

http://linkedin.com/e/abc/12345/

Please don't hesitate to contact me if you have any questions.

Thank you for your consideration.

Sincerely,

Alison Doyle

There's also a standard note to my connection:

John,

I am applying for a job I found on LinkedIn, and would sincerely appreciate it if you could take a moment to write a short recommendation for me, which you can then forward on to the job poster.

You can find details of the job I am applying for here:

http://linkedin.com/e/abc/12345/

Please let me know if you have any questions, and thank you very much.

Sincerely,

Alison Doyle

Both the templates (and any templates on LinkedIn) can be personalized and edited to fit your circumstances.

UXBRIDGE COLLEGE
LEARNING CENTRE

With the jobs that are provided by SimplyHired, you can click on "Who Do I Know?" to see if you have any connections at the company. Again, you will see how you are connected to the hiring manager and can use your connections to assist with your application.

Getting Found on LinkedIn

As well as looking for jobs, recruiters are looking for you on LinkedIn. It works both ways. Jason Alba, CEO of JibberJobber.com, says, "Recruiters refer to LinkedIn as their candidate pool. They pay a lot of money, and spend a lot of time, looking for the right person to fill a job (or looking for someone who knows someone). One of your main goals is to be found by the recruiter, even if they don't have a job for you. Make sure you are easy to find (flesh out your profile), and easy to contact. Putting in keywords, abbreviations, and details will raise the chances you are found when the recruiter is searching."

More on LinkedIn

In another situation, one of my connections asked me for a LinkedIn referral for a job he applied for. I was able to recommend him for the job to the hiring manager using LinkedIn's messaging system. This led to his resume (and his LinkedIn profile) getting a closer look and moved him into contention for the position.

Jason Alba's book *I'm on LinkedIn—Now What???* is full of excellent advice on what you can do with LinkedIn and how it can assist you. It will help you get the most out of LinkedIn and use it to your best advantage.

Staying in Touch

LinkedIn, Facebook, and Twitter are also good ways to stay in touch with your connections. I've kept the same email addresses forever, but some people change them almost as often as the wind blows. You won't have to worry about bounced email or keeping track of changed email addresses; you can simply message directly through the system.

Strategies to Build Your Network

Network building is not only fun, it's easy. I spend a few minutes every now and then checking Facebook and LinkedIn for new connections, so I can expand my network. I have about a one thousand connections, but I know people who have hundreds more. There are over 85 million LinkedIn users and 500 million Facebook users, and that's only two of the top networking sites. Think about all those people who have the potential to be useful to your job search!

When I find someone who would be a good connection, all I need to do is click to send them an invitation. Hopefully, they accept. That's why it makes sense not to abuse the system, attempting to connect with people you have nothing in common with and vice versa.

The fun part is finding people that I had lost track of. It's interesting to see who is doing what and where they've been along the way. Some people end up at jobs I never would have expected. Someone who wrote a guest article for me on Alaskan fishing jobs when I first started the About.com Job Searching site (http://jobsearch.about.com) is now vice president of a major international corporation. I would have lost touch, but we connected on LinkedIn and I've been able to stay informed about his career.

Work Your Connections

One really good way to build your network is to proactively and positively work your connections. Did someone you know just get promoted or get hired for a new job? Send them a quick congratulatory message. Has someone helped you with your job search? Send them a thank you note. It only takes a few minutes.

Write a LinkedIn Recommendation for someone you have worked with. The recommendations you have written and the ones you have received both show on your profile (if you opt to make them visible). Writing a reference is a good way to get someone to reciprocate. Those recommendations can be read by hiring managers using LinkedIn for recruiting and by your connections, so in a way, you have provided a reference in advance for a future employer.

Top Networking Sites

Where are the best sites to network? We all have many networking opportunities—including college and company alumni associations, professional associations, and social networking sites—that we can take advantage of. Regardless of your career field or interests, there is a group or association available online to network with. For example, there are networking groups for advertising executives, cancer survivors, 40+ job seekers, scientists, ministers, and veterans. That's just the tip of the iceberg.

Alumni Associations

If you're a college student or graduate, check with your school to see if they have an alumni network. If they do, you will be able to get in touch with alumni, and sometimes parents, who have volunteered to assist students and other alumni. There are college general alumni networking groups, as well as college networks specifically designed to help with internships, job searching, and business networking.

In addition to the school's own groups, there are public college networking sites, like MyWorkster and many Facebook and LinkedIn groups, designed to facilitate communications among university communities, including staff, students, and alumni.

In addition to your college alumni association, Kay Stout, of Oklahoma Professional Search (http://www.oklahomaprofessionalsearch.com) and author of the Another Point of View blog (http://anotherpointofview.typepad.com), notes that "the next best connection investment is your Social Greek organization or special interest group—think Pi Sigma Alpha (Political Science), Psi Chi (Psychology), Sigma Delta Pi (Spanish), Beta Beta Beta (Biology), etc. Why? Because when you send an electronic (or snail mail) message to someone who went to the same university as you and belonged to the same organization, there is an immediate connection. The subject line of your email should be the university or special interest group and the year you graduated (University of Colorado alum, 2007). If you share the same industry occupation, that's like a home run."

Many companies also have alumni associations. Job-hunt.org (http://tinyurl.com/4scr4bu) [job-hunt.org/employer_alumni_networking.shtml] has compiled a list of alumni and military networking groups. Adobe, the U.S. Army, Bell Labs, Deloitte & Touche, IBM, and Six Flags all have alumni groups, just to mention a few. Smaller organizations are also listed, so if you don't see your company on the list, search for it on Google: "Company Name alumni group," or take a look at the Yahoo! Groups list of Groups about Former Employees (http://tinyurl.com/457okrt) [finance.dir.groups.yahoo.com/dir/1600528678]. There are over 1,400 groups listed.

Bright Circles (http://www.brightcircles.com) is a networking site where current and former employees from leading companies and organizations are able to stay in touch.

Professional Associations

Do you belong to a professional association? Many associations have members-only networking, so check with your association(s) if you belong. If you don't, joining an association can have many benefits. The ASAE (American Society of Association Executives) has a searchable directory of associations (http://asaecenter.org) you can use to find relevant associations to join.

Social and Professional Networking Sites

LinkedIn Groups (http://learn.linkedin.com/groups/) is another good place to connect. Categories include Alumni, Corporate, Conference, Networking, Non-Profit, and Professional groups. Members can opt to let other group members contact them directly via LinkedIn's message system, so it's easy to communicate.

Facebook is very user-friendly. You can find friends, both new ones and contacts, in the networks you belong to. Friends can message friends from within Facebook, so you don't even have to send an email to talk to someone.

Social Recruiting on Job Boards

To take social networking a step further, job boards CareerBuilder and Dice have integrated social recruiting into their sites. CareerBuilder's Talent Network includes social media, personalized job recommendations, employee referrals, and a mobile-friendly interface so you can stay connected.

Employers can invite candidates to join their Talent Network from Facebook. CareerBuilder's new Facebook referral app, Work@, makes it easy for workers to identify which Facebook friends are good a match for open positions within their company and to share those opportunities with their friends.

Dice, the leading technology job site, has Talent Network where tech job seekers can connect directly with recruiters. Employers and candidates can directly connect on Dice via a message center, real-time chat, an instant message tool, and email.

KODA.us is a job site with a different angle on social networking. It's like a hybrid of the social Facebook and professional LinkedIn. Like Facebook, user profiles have photos. Users can connect with companies and vice versa.

The integration between networking and recruiting has just started and job sites will continue to develop applications that directly connect job seekers with hiring managers. It's important to take advantage of these resources because they will help you make a personal connection with a company representative, which is invaluable when you're seeking employment.

College Student/Alumni Networks

- 85 Broads

- Alumni.net

- College/university private networks (check with your school)

- Experience

- Facebook Groups

- LinkedIn Groups
- MyWorkster

Company Alumni Network Directories/Groups
- Facebook Groups
- Job-Hunt.org
- LinkedIn Groups
- Riley Guide
- Yahoo! Groups

Professional Associations
- American Society of Association Executives

Professional Networking Sites
- Bright Circles
- Doostang
- LinkedIn
- Ryze
- Spoke

Social Networking Sites
- Facebook
- Ning
- Twitter

Choose Your Networks

Obviously, you can't join every network. If you did, you wouldn't have time for anything else. There are too many of them. The key is to be selective. Pick networking sites where it's easy to manage your profiles and to connect. Choose sites that are easy to use, as well relevant to your interests and goals.

Start small and join a network or two, see how it works for you, then go on from there. Sign up for email alerts of new messages, posts, or changes in your contacts' status, so you don't have to remember to check your network(s) for what's new.

RELATED RESOURCES

- Career Networking Sites (http://tinyurl.com/24ld2h) [jobsearch.about.com/od/networkingsites/Career_ and_Social_Networking_Sites.htm]
- Top Social Networking Tips (http://tinyurl.com/2ehvnj9) [jobsearch.about.com/od/onlinecareernetworking/tp/socialne tworkingtips.htm]

---

3 Resumes and Cover Letters

Creating a Resume

Unless you're applying for job that doesn't require a resume, you will need to create an excellent resume and a cover letter. The "excellent" is the important part. Your resume and your letters need to be perfect. They need to look good, read well, and convince the employer that they need to interview you.

In fact, you should edit your resume and write a customized cover letter for each and every job you apply for. I know that sounds like a lot of work. It is. But, if you want to make a good impression on the hiring manager (and you only have a few seconds to make that impression), you need to have both a resume and a cover letter that show why you are qualified for the job and are an excellent candidate at first glance.

Perfect means no typos or grammatical errors. It's really hard to proofread your own writing. I know for a fact that I can't do it. I see the words on the page as I think I wrote them, not how they really look. So ask someone else to review your materials before you send them. Don't rely on spell check or grammar check to catch the mistakes for you. If you wrote the wrong word, *you're* instead of *your* or *principle* instead of *principal*, for example, it's not going to catch it.

What's in your resume is as important as how it looks. You need to make a strong positive impression in a very short amount of time. If you need help writing a resume, there is a lot of information available online. There are also products and people who will help write or review your resume for you.

Resume Writing Help

- Resume Writing Guide (http://tinyurl.com/2arg3d) [jobsearch.about.com/od/resumes/a/resumetoc.htm]

- Resume Writing Books (http://tinyurl.com/o5gkx) [jobsearch.about.com/od/toppicks/tp/resumewriting.htm]

- Resume Writing/Reviewing Services (http://tinyurl.com/d2vv8z) [jobsearch.about.com/od/resumeservices/a/resumewriting.htm]

- College Career Services Offices

It's always helpful to review resume samples. I have a selection on the About.com Job Searching site (http://jobsearch.about.com) that you can take a look at.

Resume Content

There is basic content that should be included in every resume:

- **Contact information:** name, address, phone, email

- **Experience:** positions, employers, and a description of what you did at each job

- **Education:** colleges attended and graduation dates

- **Skills:** skills relevant to the jobs you are applying for

Sample Resume Format

Contact Information

First Name, Last Name
Home Street Address
Home City, State, Zip
Home Phone
Cell Phone
Email Address

Career Highlights (optional)

This section of your resume lists the skills and experience that are specifically related to the job for which you are applying.

Experience

The experience section of your resume includes your work history. List in reverse chronological order (most recent first): your employer, the dates of employment, the positions held, along with a bulleted list of your job responsibilities and your accomplishments.

Company Name
City, State
Dates of Employment
Job Title
Responsibilities

Education

College, Degree
Awards, Honors

Skills

List the skills related to the position for which you are applying—for example, programming, software, or language skills.

The Details Matter

Contact Information: Make sure all your contact information is accurate. Believe it or not, I know people who have put the wrong phone number or an email address that they no longer use on their resume. Even though they had good credentials, there is no way they could be reached to schedule an interview.

Phone Number: List a phone number that you can check frequently for messages. When a recruiter calls you, they want to speak to you sooner rather than later.

Email Address: Don't use an AOL email address when applying for a tech job. As one employer told me, AOL users are considered low-tech. Do make sure your email address sounds professional (don't use *cool-cat@mail.com*, *hotchick@gmail.com*, etc.—you get the idea). Your name is always appropriate to use for your email address. For example, I have several variations like adoyle, alisondoyle, etc. with the email accounts I use.

Formatting: Use a simple, easy-to-read font on your resume such as Times New Roman or Verdana. Don't make it too large or too small. Nobody wants to have to squint to read a resume. Leave plenty of white space between your content. If you need to go beyond one page, that's fine. It's better to have a readable resume than a jam-packed one that is hard to read.

Writing: Be specific. Highlight your achievements (e.g., "I increased sales revenue 120% for fiscal year 2007") and your qualifications. Be brief; use bullets and short sentences. No prospective employer wants to read a book.

The Truth Matters

I have lost track of how many frantic emails I have received saying, "I fudged the dates I worked at my last company and now I have a job offer, but they are conducting a background check. What do I do?" Or, "Even though I attended college for three and a half years, I didn't graduate, although I said I did on my resume. What do I do now?"

When that happens, you have a problem. You can come clean with the recruiter and tell them that you made a "mistake" on your resume or hope you don't get caught. Do keep in mind that even if you don't get caught, you can get fired at any point in the future (sometimes years later) if the company finds out you lied on your resume.

It's much less stressful to be honest. Tell the truth on your resume, on your job applications, and in your cover letters, and your lies won't come back to haunt you down the road.

Age-Proof Your Resume

In a competitive job market, age is definitely a hiring issue. It's important to age-proof your resume so hiring managers see you as a competitive candidate, not someone who is "too old" to be considered for employment.

If you haven't updated your resume in a while, give your resume a makeover. Take a look at samples (http://tinyurl.com/rpvdy) [jobsearch.about.com/od/sampleresumes/a/sampleresume2.htm] and choose a style and design that is modern and professional.

You don't need to include all your experience on your resume, especially if you have been employed for many years. It's acceptable to limit the related experience you include on your resume to the last fifteen years.

There is no need to include dates in the Education section of your resume. High school and college graduation dates can be left off your resume. If you have a college degree, don't include your high school on your resume.

Show that your skills are current. Include the latest programs you're familiar with and leave out-of-date technology off your resume. If you have taken classes to update your skills, include them on your resume.

Targeted Resumes

A targeted resume is a resume that is written to show that you are specifically qualified for the job you are applying for. When writing a targeted resume, you match your skills and experience to the qualifications listed in the help wanted ad or job posting.

You can target your resume either by including a Career Highlights or Summary of Qualifications section at the top of your resume or by rewriting your resume to focus on your qualifications for the job. Either way, it's important to show the hiring manager that you have the qualifications he or she needs.

If you are struggling to make the case that you're qualified for a job, reconsider applying. Applying for jobs you're not qualified for is not only a waste of the employer's time, it's a waste of your time as well. I've received resumes from someone with a background in childcare who was applying for a C++ programmer position and from a former CEO for an administrative assistant position. One was clearly under qualified, and the other overqualified. Neither one had a resume (or a cover letter) that indicated in any way why they might be good candidates or why they were qualified for the positions.

Resume Reviews

Once you have compiled all the information you need into a resume and have a draft ready for review, our experts in the About.com Job Searching Forum (http://jobsearch.about.com/mpboards.htm) can provide feedback and suggestions.

The Resume Black Hole

One of the things I hear most often from job seekers is that they work really hard on their resume, apply for jobs, and don't hear anything back. That resume black hole, which seems to suck in resumes regardless of how good they are, definitely exists. However, there are strategies you can use to get your resume to the top of the pile.

First of all, be sure you are applying for jobs that you are qualified for. If your credentials aren't what the company is seeking, you don't have a chance of getting an interview. There are too many applicants for every job, so only the most qualified candidates will be selected to interview.

Use resume keywords that match the skills listed in the job description. The closer the match, the better chance your resume will have of being selected by the software that companies use to screen resumes.

Take the time to write a targeted cover letter that specifies why you are a strong candidate for the job.

Writing Cover Letters

Those candidates whose resumes didn't have any qualifications for the jobs I was recruiting for could have made the case, perhaps, that they were good candidates for the jobs in their cover letters.

Instead, they said they were interested in the positions. They didn't reference why they were qualified or why they wanted the job. Letters like that won't get anyone an interview. Rather, cover letters that work explain the reasons for your interest in the company. They include the most relevant skills or experiences you have for the position you're applying for. Remember, it's not the skills you think are important that matter, it's the skills the hiring manager wants his new employee to have that are critical to securing an interview.

Consider it from the hiring manager's perspective. He wants to hire the most qualified candidate for the job, and he'll get many resumes from candidates who are qualified. Why would he consider the others? He won't, and that's why your cover letter needs to be targeted to show that you're a candidate who deserves an interview.

Julie Greenberg, cofounder of Jobnob (http://www.jobnob.com) explains: "Too often job seekers overlook the importance of a cover letter. The cover letter is your one chance to speak directly to the hiring manager or HR gatekeeper. It's literally like you've gotten sixty seconds of their time for your elevator pitch—your quick spiel about why you are so great. Yes, your resume is very important, but in a cover letter you get the opportunity to tell an employer something about who you are, how well you write, and how much you are interested in this specific job and why. You don't get to do that with a resume. So the rule to follow is: If you are submitting a resume, you should be submitting a cover letter. Always."

Targeted Cover Letters

A targeted cover letter, just like a targeted resume, specifically relates your experience to the job posting you are applying for. You need to write a customized letter for every job you are interested in.

Sample Cover Letter Format

Your Contact Information

First Name, Last Name
Home Street Address
Home City, State, Zip
Home Phone Number
Cell Phone Number
Email Address

Date

Company Contact Information

(Leave out if you don't have the information)

Name
Job Title
Company
Street Address
City, State, Zip Code

Salutation

(Leave out if you don't have the information)

Dear Mr./Ms. Last Name:

First Paragraph

The first paragraph of your cover letter lets the hiring manager know what position you are applying for. Include the name of a contact at the company, if you have one.

Middle Paragraphs

The middle section of your cover letter explains why you are qualified for the job. You need to convince the recruiter that you should be scheduled for an interview. Connect your skills and abilities with the qualifications listed in the job posting. Specify how your experience is a strong match for the job. Use bullets or short paragraphs.

Final Paragraph

The final paragraph thanks the employer for considering you for the job. You can also include information on how you will follow up, as long as the job posting doesn't specify "no phone calls."

Complimentary Close

Sincerely,

Signature

Typed name for a letter sent via email or uploaded online, or hand-written signature for a mailed letter.

Review Sample Cover Letters

It's always helpful to review sample cover letters to get ideas for what to write and how to format your letter. I have a collection available on my About.com Job Searching site (http://jobsearch.about.com) and there are plenty of other samples available in cover letter writing books and online.

The Elements of Resume Style: Essential Rules and Eye-Opening Advice for Writing Resumes and Cover Letters that Work by Scott Bennett is a little book full of good advice for resume and cover letter writing.

Joyce Lain Kennedy's *Cover Letters for Dummies* and *Resumes for Dummies* are both good resources for resume and letter writing, as well. They provide advice on how to write resumes and letters, samples, as well as tips and suggestions for writing resumes and cover letters.

One of my favorite cover letter samples is shown below. The candidate specifically related the job requirements to her skills. It's very clear, at first glance, to the employer that she's qualified for the job. This letter not only got her an interview, it also got her a job offer.

Requirements

- Responsible for administrative operations in college student affairs office, including managing program registration, solving customer problems, dealing with risk management and emergencies, and establishment and enforcement of department policies.

- Hiring, training, and supervision of staff, including supervision of student workers and graduate interns.

- Strong interpersonal skills are required.

- Valid New York driver's license with good driving record. Ability to travel to different offices required.

- Extensive experience in undergraduate collegiate programming creation, organization, and management required.

Qualifications

- Manage student registration for college courses, design and manage program administration software, solve customer problems, create and enforce department policy, and serve as a liaison between office administration and students, faculty, and staff

- Emergency planning managing training and certification

- Hiring, training, scheduling and management of staff; managing and ordering supply inventory

- New York driver's license with NTSA defensive driving certification

- Extensive experience in collegiate programming design, implementation, and management

---

TIPS FOR WRITING COVER LETTERS

- Cover letter is targeted, concise, clear, logical, and well organized.
- Letter specifically relates your qualifications to the job.
- Use your cover letter to explain any gaps in your employment.
- Proofread and then have someone else review the letter for you.
- Read your letter out loud to make sure there are no missing words.
- Keep a copy for your records.

Sending Your Resume and Letters

How to send your letter depends on whether you are mailing it via the USPS or sending it via email or applying online. If you're mailing your application materials, print your cover letter on white (or off-white) bond paper that matches your resume. Don't forget to sign it. Either mail it flat or fold with the letter on top over the resume.

Sending via Email

When you apply via email, there are a couple of options. You can write your cover letter directly into an email message (the same rules for writing a proper letter and proofing it apply) and attach your resume (a MS Word attachment is best). Or you can attach both your resume and letter as separate documents to the email message. Send yourself a copy as well (use the bcc field in your email program). That way you'll have a copy for your records.

When you send your cover letter in the body of the email address, be sure to include your contact information (email address, phone number, etc.) in your signature, so it's easy for the hiring manager to get in touch with you.

Name Your Resume: Save a copy of your resume, including your name in the document name, e.g., AlisonDoyleResume.doc (Your-NameResume.doc). That way your resume can be easily identified by the hiring manager.

Subject Line of Message: Should include the position you're applying for and your name. Example: Credit Suisse Analyst/Alison Doyle.

Signature: Include your contact information (email address, phone number, etc.) in your signature, so it's easy for the hiring manager to get in touch with you.

Applying Online

Applying online via a job site, like Monster or CareerBuilder, or directly on a company's website, is simple. All you need to do is follow the directions. You will either upload your resume or copy/paste the information from your resume into an online resume builder or application. There also may be an option to upload a cover letter. Again, follow the instructions and they will walk you through the process.

What (and What Not) to Do

Do follow the directions. Employers want you to do what they ask and they don't have much tolerance for applicants who don't follow the rules. If the job posting says send your resume as a PDF file, don't send a Word document, convert it. You can do that online (search for Word to PDF conversion) if you don't have software to convert the file for you. If the directions say include a cover letter, write one or you won't be considered for the job.

Be very careful. The auto-fill option that is built into many email programs (where the program fills in the email address of who it thinks you are writing to) is dangerous. I know job seekers who weren't paying attention and ended up sending their resume to their boss by mistake. That's one reason why using a dedicated email account just for job searching makes sense.

Do not send a resume without a message. I've received way too many random resumes attached to an email message. In some cases, I have no clue why the person is sending them to me or what they expect me to do with them. Make sure your email message is clear about why you are sending the resume and what job you are applying for.

Don't use your work email account. It's not only not smart to use your work email account to apply for jobs because many companies monitor employee email activity, it also won't make a good impression with prospective employers. How do they know you won't do the same thing in the future and use their equipment, software, and time to apply for your next job?

Do not use a spam blocker. A spam blocker requires people who aren't in your address book to go online and fill out a form before they can send you a message. That happened to me the other day when I was responding to someone who had written to me at my About.com Job Searching email address. She said she desperately needed advice, so I took the time to respond only to get an email message saying I need to be an approved sender to write to her. Making a potential employer (or someone giving you advice or help) jump through hoops to respond to you is a really bad idea. Most people won't bother.

Saying Thank You

Following up after an interview with a thank you letter is a very important part of the application process. Hiring managers think more highly of applicants who take the time to thank them for the interview and to reiterate their interest in the position.

Susan Heathfield, the About.com Guide to Human Resources, explains, "The interview thank you letter is a small gold mine of information for the employer. It's one more piece in the puzzle about matching the most qualified candidate to the employer's job. Since this is the application material least likely to be reviewed by others before sending, spelling, grammar, and typos matter because the employer is observing your writing skills and your attention to detail. The employer is also confirming that you understood their communication about the job, the company, and the interviewers. The employer wants to hear your enthusiasm and interest in the position. And, when you recap your skills in the thank you letter, it gives the employer one more opportunity to note the match between what you bring and what the job requires."

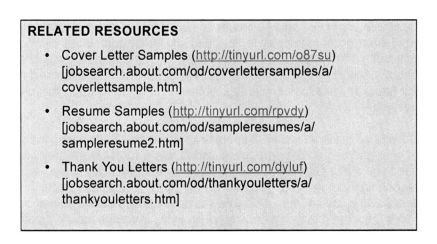

RELATED RESOURCES

- Cover Letter Samples (http://tinyurl.com/o87su) [jobsearch.about.com/od/coverlettersamples/a/coverlettsample.htm]

- Resume Samples (http://tinyurl.com/rpvdy) [jobsearch.about.com/od/sampleresumes/a/sampleresume2.htm]

- Thank You Letters (http://tinyurl.com/dyluf) [jobsearch.about.com/od/thankyouletters/a/thankyouletters.htm]

Chapter 3: Resumes and Cover Letters

4 How to Job Search Online

How to Start a Job Search

One of the hardest parts of beginning a job search is to know where to start. The Internet has more job sites than you can count, and starting and managing a job search can be complicated. You can't just go to Google and search for "jobs" because you'll get more results (over a billion at this point in time) than you'll know what to do with. Some may be relevant to your job search, most won't be.

There are job banks; job search engines that search the Internet for listings and aggregate jobs from multiple sites; niche job sites that focus on a specific career field or geographic area; networking sites where you can connect with hiring managers and where recruiters can find you; and ways, like writing a blog, to create an online presence that helps build your career.

You may need to use some of these resources; others won't be necessary. What's important is to keep your job search as uncomplicated as possible. The simpler it is, the more effective it will be.

Before you do anything at all, you will need to decide what type of job you're looking for. That helps simplify the process. If you're looking for a job close to home, for example, you can focus on the local job search sites.

That's exactly what Priscilla did. She was a part-time graduate student who was looking for a part-time job to pay the bills. She visited her local Chamber of Commerce website and saw a couple of postings that looked like they would be a fit. She uploaded her resume and applied. Within a few hours she was called to schedule an interview. She interviewed that very same day and got a job offer the next morning.

Of course, it's not always that easy. There's more work involved if you're looking for a professional position, want to relocate, don't have the best work history, or want to change careers. However, if you start with one resource at a time and build your job search, it will be much easier. There is no point in trying to learn everything and in using resources you don't need.

Joe, for example, is a pharmaceutical sales representative. When he was laid off from his job, he decided he wanted to stay in the same line of work and wanted to stay in the Atlanta area, where he lived. Rather than posting his resume on every job board he could find, he targeted several pharmaceutical firms. He applied directly to those companies via the company websites. He networked with clients, former colleagues, and members of the local professional associations. Joe also used LinkedIn to find contacts at the companies where he wanted to work. He was able to skip some steps in the process because his job search was so focused.

So, before you begin your job search you need a plan. You need to have at least some ideas about what you want to do. You also need a resume and to be prepared to write a cover letter for each of the jobs you apply for.

Job Search Plan

There are also some basic tools you will need to conduct a job search. Access to a computer and an email account you can use for job searching are a must. It helps to have a dedicated email you can use so your job search correspondence doesn't get jumbled with your personal correspondence. Also:

- Decide what type of job you want (industry, career field, full-time, part-time)

- Decide where you want to work (geographic area)

- Write a resume or be prepared to complete job applications

- Find job listings

- Write cover letters

- Apply online

- Follow up

- Use your contacts (networking)

Email Accounts

Free web-based email services are available (Gmail, Yahoo!) and if you use one, you will be able to check your email from wherever you are. You will also be able to set up folders where you can keep copies of the resumes you have sent and the correspondence that needs follow-up.

Store Your Documents

Set up a job search folder on your computer. Keep copies of the resumes and letters you have sent, so the information will be readily available when you start receiving calls to schedule interviews. Also keep a copy of the emails you send.

You can also store your job search documents online. Upload your resume and cover letters to Google Docs and you will be able to access them from any web browser. That way, you'll have everything you need to apply for your jobs available on any computer.

There are also websites specifically designed for storing and sending your resume. ResumeBucket (http://www.resumebucket.com) users can upload their resume directly from their computer or create a resume online with the resume building service. You'll get a unique URL just for your resume.

Josh Stomel, Founder of ResumeBucket.com and NeoHire.com, explains why it's important to have a copy of your resume online: "When your resume is on the web, you can update it at any moment, instantly. You can edit, modify, and update your resume in seconds making sure anyone browsing through it has all of your current qualifications. An uploaded resume has the potential to be seen by millions of people in your local area, the nation, and even the world. Just years ago it would have been impossible to network your resume the way you can today on the web."

Storing your resume online will enable you to apply for any job, any time, regardless of where you are. That can give you a competitive edge, because the first candidates to apply for jobs often get a closer look than the others. That's especially true when employers receive hundreds of applications for every open position, and that's happening more and more frequently.

A Place to Work

If you don't have a computer, your local public library may have computers you can use for free. Or, try an Internet café. Though it's easier if you have your own computer, both of these are feasible options, because you can conduct just about every facet of your job search via the Internet.

A dedicated place to work on your job search activities is important, even if it is only a corner of your kitchen table. You need a place for your computer and your phone. You'll also need a planner (online or paper), notepad, and pen so you're prepared when you get called for an interview.

Be sure to have a quiet place to talk on the phone. Recruiters don't need to hear dogs and kids in the background when they are trying to talk to you about a job. If the timing isn't right to have a conversation, ask if you could schedule a time to talk later or on the next day.

Job Search Tools

Consider using a job search management tool such as JibberJobber (http://jibberjobber.com) to manage your activities online and keep track of where you have applied, whom you have contacted, and what you need to do next.

An Excel spreadsheet works, too. Set up columns for:

- Company Name

- Date Resume Sent

- Contact Person

- Follow-Up Date

- Notes

Another option is the contact manager that comes with some email programs, like Microsoft Outlook. Regardless of what product you use, you need to be able to keep track of your job applications and the people who are helping you with them.

Get all the tools you need in place before you start. It's much easier to apply for jobs when you're organized, than when you have to run to the store to get paper for your printer or to the post office to get stamps, so you can get a resume in the mail.

Very Useful Job Search Tools

- Computer

- Printer

- Phone (land line or cell phone) with voicemail

- Email address

- Organizer/planner

- Contact manager

- Paper

- Mailing envelopes

- Stamps

Get Organized

Set aside some time to work on your job search. Job searching really is a whole lot like work and it's going to take dedicated effort to find a new position. One thing to keep in mind is that most people don't look for jobs on the weekend. So, if you can spend a few weekend hours on your job search, you'll have an edge over other applicants and your application may be among the first ones the hiring manager sees on Monday morning.

Review Job Options

If you're not sure what type of job you want, take some time to review job options. The days of deciding what you want to do when you grow up and sticking with that for your working life are over. Now, it's more a question of what to do next.

That's especially true in a difficult economy where jobs are being cut, entire industries have been decimated, and the job market is as competitive as it has ever been.

If your skills aren't quite as marketable as they used to be, consider how you can transfer them to another job, industry, or career field. Transferable skills are all the skills (from school, work, volunteering, activities, continuing education, etc.) that you have that can be used for employment purposes. It's important to use those skills to your best advantage when you're job searching.

Willy Franzen, Founder of One Day One Job (http://onedayonejob.com), says, "If you can step out of your job search and start thinking about what companies, products, and ideas excite you and what problems you want to work to solve, then you can start to get creative with your job search. There's no better tool than the Internet to help you generate these ideas and then research them to determine whether they might lead to job search prospects."

There are websites that can help you figure out what your transferable skills are and what you can do with them during the next phase of your career.

Use Monster's Career Snapshots (http://tinyurl.com/d3u45v) [my.monster.com/Job-Profiles/GetProfile.aspx] to explore thousands of different jobs that match your interests and skills. Then, use Monster's Career Mapping Tool (http://tinyurl.com/cc32ax) [my.monster.com/Career-Planning/Pathing.aspx#tabIndex=0&path=& eview=H] to take a look at the career paths that will get you to the careers you're considering.

Get Help

If you're not sure about what you want to do or are having difficulty with your job search, remember that there is help available. If you're a college student or graduate, your career services office may be able to assist.

There are career counselors and coaches who can provide assistance. Visit the National Career Development Association (http://www.ncda.org) for a list of certified counselors in your area. Many State Department of Labor offices provide workshops and assistance for job seekers as well.

Be Active

You need to actively work at your job search. One job seeker lost an opportunity for what could have been a dream job because he didn't check his email in a timely manner. By the time he got around to checking it, someone else had been hired.

One of my pet peeves is when job seekers complain that nothing is happening with their job search. Those are often the people who wait a week or so to apply, don't respond to email from recruiters and contacts, and don't follow up in a timely manner. If you want the job, you need to be among the first to apply, the first to respond, the first to send a thank you letter after an interview—you get the idea.

Davidia, for example, spent a week mulling over her resume, a cover letter, and a writing sample. By the time she had gotten it just right, it was too late. The employer had a full interview schedule and wasn't considering any further applications. That old saying, "He who hesitates is lost," holds true when it comes to looking for a job. Recruiters don't want to wait around for someone who isn't responsive or proactive.

☐ *Apply Immediately.* Don't wait to apply for jobs that match your specifications.

☐ *Check Email.* Check at least twice a day, early in the morning and mid-afternoon, so you can respond the same day you received the message.

☐ *Respond to Email.* Answer recruiter and contact email immediately.

☐ *Telephone.* Check for messages throughout the day (if you're working, check your voicemail during breaks and/or your lunch hour).

☐ *Mail.* Check your mail—you may get a letter or postcard asking you to call to schedule an interview.

☐ *Networking Sites.* Reach out to contacts and respond to messages from anyone who is helping you with your job search in a timely manner.

Also, update your online accounts on a regular basis. Kellie Morris, Senior IT Auditor at aigDirect.com, notes, "When I am actively searching, I repost my resume every five to seven days. It gives the appearance that I have not been looking a long time."

How to Apply for Jobs Online

There isn't any room for guesswork in applying for jobs online. It's really simple. Follow the instructions in the job posting. Companies think less of (or will ignore) applicants who don't follow the instructions. If the listing says send a cover letter, write one. If the listing says apply online at CareerBuilder, do so. When the help wanted ad says send a PDF, don't send a Word document.

How Employers Accept Applications

- Directly at their company website

- By email, to a general human resources email box or to an individual

- From a job site (you will have uploaded your resume to the site)

- By mail

Follow the instructions in the job posting. Keep track, as I said, of where you applied, so you can manage your job search.

Online Job Applications

When companies want you to apply for jobs at the company website, you will probably need to complete an online application rather than submitting your resume. That's because the company is using a hiring system that tracks applicants from the time they apply to the time they get hired.

The easiest way to complete these applications is to copy and paste the information from your resume into the application. If there's an option to upload your cover letter, write a letter, then paste it into the box provided.

How to Follow Up

Following up when you have applied for a job online can be tricky. Many companies don't list a contact person because they don't want to be bombarded with phone calls and emails. They want to follow up with those candidates they are interested in and not have to deal with the rest.

There is a school of thought that believes you should track down a contact person (hiring manager, supervisor, etc.) and follow up on your application, regardless of what's listed in the help wanted ad. I don't think that makes sense. It's better to be respectful of the employer's wishes and if the ad says *no calls*, don't call. Rather, follow up with an email a week or so after you've submitted your materials to check on the status of your application.

Sample Follow-Up Letter

Dear Mr./Ms. Last Name:
(Omit this line if you don't have a contact person's name)

I submitted a resume two weeks ago for the marketing assistant position you advertised on Craigslist.

I am very interested in working at ABC Company, and my skills, especially my sales and marketing experience at DEF company, are an excellent match for this opportunity.

I would be glad to resend my resume or to provide any further information you might need regarding my candidacy. I can be reached at (555) 555-5555 or at jdoe@email.com.

I look forward to hearing from you.

Sincerely,

Your name

Follow-Up Timing

When you follow up by email, send a message a week or two after you applied. Unless the message bounced, (and if it did you'll get a copy in your email inbox), presume that the recruiter or hiring manager got it. Don't bombard them with email messages.

If you follow up with a phone call, try to call early in the morning. People are more likely to pick up their phone before they are caught up in a busy workday. Again, call a week or so after you applied.

Todd Lempicke, President of Optimal Resume, says, "There should be a least three attempts at following up including phone and email. It should be much more than just checking to see if the resume was received. The voice mail message could be an abbreviated elevator speech, and the follow up letter could summarize all of the ways in which they are qualified. LinkedIn can be a great tool for following up too. Every job sought requires research and its own follow up strategy."

When You Don't Hear Back

Unfortunately, many employers are really bad at following up. I know people who have sent hundreds of resumes and only received a few replies. If you don't hear back soon after applying, follow up, and if you still don't get a response, forget it.

The trend is for companies to follow up only with candidates they are interested in. In the past, you'd get a letter or a postcard saying the job was filled. Now, you're lucky if you get an email. Part of the reason is that with the changeover to online recruiting, there are many more applications than are manageable for every job opening.

If you have a connection at the company, ask him or her if they can check on the status of your resume. They may also be able to give it a closer look and get you into contention for the job.

Don't feel badly if you don't get a response, even though it is annoying when you put a lot of work into your cover letter and you think the job is perfect for you. Your idea of perfect may not come close to the employer's vision of the perfect employee. This is the nature of the job search business. Right or wrong, that's how it works.

Don't Stop and Don't Wait

There is a danger when you've sent a couple of resumes, when the interviews start trickling in, and when it looks like you might get an offer, to stop and wait to see what happens. What's dangerous is that you don't know for certain that you've got a job until you have a definitive offer.

One job seeker I worked with did a really good job of juggling multiple potential jobs. She scheduled first and second interviews, delayed some when she thought she was close to getting an offer on another, and overall, she did all the right things. Then she thought she had an offer from a company, so she declined further interviews with the others and stopped sending her resume.

What she had wasn't an offer. It was a vague email saying they are interested in hiring. There was no salary mentioned, no benefits listed, nothing definitive that she should have construed as an offer that met her requirements. It took her two weeks to get an actual dollar-and-cents offer from the hiring manager. It wasn't even close to what she had expected to get and wasn't a salary she would accept under any circumstances.

The moral of the story is to keep plugging away; look for jobs, apply for jobs, interview, until you have the right (salary, benefits, perks, hours) written offer from a company that you want to work for. That's when you can consider yourself hired.

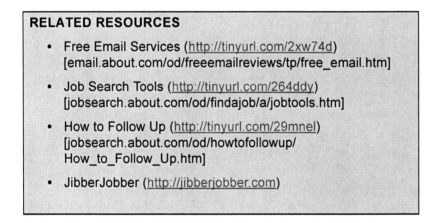

RELATED RESOURCES

- Free Email Services (http://tinyurl.com/2xw74d)
  [email.about.com/od/freeemailreviews/tp/free_email.htm]

- Job Search Tools (http://tinyurl.com/264ddy)
  [jobsearch.about.com/od/findajob/a/jobtools.htm]

- How to Follow Up (http://tinyurl.com/29mnel)
  [jobsearch.about.com/od/howtofollowup/
  How_to_Follow_Up.htm]

- JibberJobber (http://jibberjobber.com)

5 Where to Find Jobs

Where are the best places to find jobs? If you ask career experts and job seekers, you'll get a mixed bag of responses. There isn't one site that works for everyone. It depends on the type of job you're looking for and where you want to work.

I tend to like the job search engines, because you can find jobs from a variety of sources, but there are other sites that come highly recommended. Kellie Morris, Senior IT Auditor at aigDirect.com, says, "Over the last eleven years, Dice.com has been invaluable to me in finding IT openings and landing both permanent and contract positions."

Gregg Bender, Aviation Technical Writer, has had good luck with Indeed, the job search engine, and LinkedIn. He told me, "The best sites I have used are LinkedIn and Indeed.com. LinkedIn has allowed me to stay in professional touch with many former coworkers that I otherwise would have lost in the 'email shuffle.' Indeed.com seems to be the most comprehensive listing of openings, is updated rapidly, and is very user-friendly."

Latasha Hasty, Group Account Supervisor, has done well with Monster: "I've posted my resume on Monster.com in the past and received a lot of calls for legitimate opportunities in my field."

The niche (sites that focus on a specific career field or industry or type of job) job sites are recommended as well. Andrea Santiago, Healthcare Recruiter, and Health Careers Guide for About.com notes, "Industry-specific job boards such as healthcare, engineering, etc., also produce better results than the bigger, broader job boards, in my experience. The Internet is an excellent resource for gathering industry information or corporate information to use in your job search, so I recommend looking beyond the obvious job boards."

I've heard pros and cons from Craigslist users about how effective it is for job searching, but I definitely think it's worth using. Eric Hamilton, Photographer and Entrepreneur, agrees. He used Craigslist when hiring and said, "Not only did I get qualified leads from Craigslist, I got dozens and hired one of them! I have a couple more dotcom startups waiting in the wings, and when it comes time to recruit, Craigslist and LinkedIn will be the ONLY tools I use."

Using a professional association works too. Marshall Maglothin, MHA, MBA, DC Metro Executive, says, "One of the professional organizations I belong to has focused, sub-specialty listserv groups. I am VERY active in mine, and any others that indirectly relate or that I might want to explore."

In fact, I heard from a few job seekers who found a job simply by using Google and searching for their town and the type of job they were looking for. Depending on where you live, you may get too many results to search through, and the postings could be out of date, but it can't hurt to try to see if you can generate some leads.

I've also found jobs using the help wanted ads from the local newspaper. In many cases, local newspapers have classifieds on the web and, depending on the newspaper, you may be able to apply directly online.

So, in a nutshell, there isn't one place to look for jobs. There also isn't any site you shouldn't use. Pick and choose among the sites that work best for you and stick with the sites where you get good responses from recruiters and hiring managers, and sites where you find a critical mass of job openings. You want to get enough results to make your searching worthwhile.

Job Listing Sites

- Company websites

- Help wanted ads

- Job search engines

- Job banks

- Local job sites

- Niche job sites

- Networking sites

- Professional associations

Company Websites

Do you know where you want to work? If so, visit the company website frequently to check job postings, and to apply online for available opportunities. You will find the job listings in either the Careers section of the website or as a subsection of About Us. At some sites, you may be able to set up email alerts to notify you of new listings.

Company Research Sites

Next, take it one step further, and check the sites that provide information about companies and jobs at those companies. You'll be able to find out information about the prospective employers you're interested in, as well as about jobs and salaries at the company. You will also be able to find out who are connected to at the company. Those connections can help you with your application and perhaps give you a reference.

In addition, the salary information you find will be helpful when you interview. Julie Greenberg, cofounder of Jobnob (http://www.jobnob.com) explains: "Do your research before you go to an interview to learn what a company is already paying. You can talk to your headhunter or recruiter or use online sites like JobNob. So find out what the company is actually paying for the position you're interviewing for, decide how much you want the job and what you're willing to accept as a salary, and maybe push the boundary a little with your initial salary request. As long as it's reasonable, even if it's high for them, you can still be in the game and land the job you want at the right price."

Glassdoor.com (http://glassdoor.com) is another good site for researching companies. It has company reviews, ratings, salaries, CEO approval ratings, competitors, content providers, and more company information. Users can find and anonymously share company reviews, ratings and salary information for jobs at each company listed.

LinkedIn's (http://linkedin.com) company pages are a great resource for information on companies of interest. LinkedIn members can see whom they are connected to at the company, jobs that they might be interested in, and insight into employees who work at the company.

LinkedIn's Company Follow is a tool job seekers can use to research companies and to see who they are connected with at companies. Those connections at companies of interest can help you with company research and with recommending you for employment with the company.

When you follow a company, you'll see blog posts, jobs, company news, corporate twitter feeds, and more company updates.

Job Search Sites

The major job boards are still the sites where most employers post listings. So they definitely should be utilized in your job search. Just don't count on them as the only resource because almost every other online job seeker is using them, as well.

I've spoken to hiring managers who get hundreds, and sometimes thousands, of resumes every time they post a job on Monster, for example. The same holds true for the other top sites. Employers are literally inundated with applications, so it's hard to get noticed.

On the other hand, simply posting your resume can generate interest in you. Several people I know have received emails or phone calls from recruiters and hiring managers shortly after posting their resume.

Here are the top sites, along with a brief description of how they work. At most sites, job seekers can post several versions of their resume and cover letter and apply directly online. Most sites also offer job agents, so you can sign up to have new listings that meet your criteria sent via email. In addition, many sites provide extensive career resources, including salary information, company information, and career advice.

Top Job Banks

CareerBuilder.com: Job seekers can post resumes and search for jobs by city, state, industry, company, or job category. You can select which career fields you are interested in, so employers can contact you. Privacy settings are also available, so you can limit who sees your resume. CareerBuilder's matching ·technology and profile database personalizes search results for job seekers. The most relevant jobs are shown to job seekers and automatically sent as new candidate matches are discovered. CareerBuilder's Talent Network includes social media, personalized job recommendations, employee referrals, and a mobile-friendly interface.

Dice.com: Dice is the top technology job site. In addition to searching and applying for tech jobs, job seekers can utilize the Dice Talent Network. Candidates can create profiles with links to their social networking profiles, including LinkedIn, Facebook, YouTube, Twitter, and their blogs. Hiring managers and job seekers can directly connect on Dice via a message center, real-time chat, an instant message tool, as well as via email.

Monster.com: Users can search Monster by keyword, location, and job category. If you register, you will be able to set up job search agents to receive information via email on new listings that meet your search criteria. There are also a variety of specialized searches available, including health care, finance, and hourly jobs.

USAJobs.gov: This is the Federal Government's official source for federal government job listings, job applications, and employment information. Job seekers interested in applying for a government job can search for job listings and apply online.

Job Search Engines

The job search engines are a good way to get your job search off to a fast start. They work a little differently than the traditional job sites. Rather than listing jobs posted by employers, they are set up so users can search the entire Internet (or most of it) in one step. The job search engines search the top job sites, company websites, associations, and other sources of job listings.

G.L. Hoffman, Chairman of LinkUp.com, says, "There are so many jobs on most of the job boards and aggregators that the job seeker is increasingly frustrated with finding real openings. The number one complaint by the job seeker is that companies do not acknowledge receipt of the cover letter and resume, usually because the HR department is overworked and understaffed to the point of not being able to even do business in a courteous manner. That is precisely why we developed LinkUp.com; our idea was to find and share (for free) only jobs that a company posts on its own website."

The basic search is by keyword and location. Advanced Search options typically include type of position, company, radius of a specific location, and when the job was posted.

Most job search engines generate a list in your browser. You can also set up job search agents. New job postings matching the search criteria you set up are emailed to you.

You may need to look carefully through the results to find listings that meet your needs, but these sites are resources that should be included on your list of job search sites to be checked regularly.

The job search engines sites do more than just find job listings. They also include "add-on" features you can use to find information about the company listing the position, the job, or the salary.

Top Job Search Engines

Indeed.com: Indeed includes millions of job listings from thousands of websites, including company career pages, job boards, newspaper classifieds, associations, and blogs. Any job search can be saved as an email alert, so new jobs are delivered daily. Job seekers may also search job trends and salaries, read and participate in discussion forums, research companies, and even find people working for companies of interest through their online social networks.

LinkUp.com: LinkUp searches jobs directly from company sites. The job postings are from small, mid-sized, and large company career sections. Because the jobs are coming directly from the employer, they are typically open positions.

SimplyHired.com: SimplyHired searches job boards, classified ads, and company sites. Advanced search options include type of job, type of company, keyword, location, and the job posting date. Simply-Hired.com's "Who Do I Know?" application that lets users view who they are connected with on Facebook and LinkedIn when they search for jobs on SimplyHired.

Niche Job Search Engines

Niche job search engines search for more specialized job postings than the general job search engines do. For example, Green Job Spider allows job seekers to search over fifty job boards that focus on green jobs. JobsOnTheMenu.com has restaurant and food service job opportunities. TwitJobSearch.com searches Twitter for job postings.

I have a directory of niche job search engines on my About.com Job Search site (http://tinyurl.com/47kqhtd) [jobsearch.about.com/od/nichejobsearchengines/Niche_Job_Search_Engines.htm] that you can consult to find niche job search engines related to your career field or industry.

Local Job Search

Your local job search sites (focused on a specific geographic area) can be a treasure trove of job listings. My local Chamber of Commerce, for example, has a free job listing service for member companies. They can post jobs online and job seekers can apply via email.

There is often less competition on sites that are smaller and visited less frequently. Not everyone knows they are there and there aren't always a large number of local qualified applicants. I know several people who applied via that Chamber of Commerce website I mentioned who heard within hours of applying regarding scheduling an interview.

The same holds true for helped wanted ads from your local newspaper and for small company websites that are seeking local or regional candidates. Because they aren't hiring on a national basis, they are interested in finding local candidates who they can hire relatively quickly.

Networking Sites

I've spoken to many hiring managers and recruiters who have had success finding qualified candidates on LinkedIn. Recruiter Andrea Santiago told me, "I have had much better luck finding jobs or finding people for my jobs or my clients' jobs through professional association sites and networking sites such as LinkedIn, etc. I've used LinkedIn as a networking tool for qualified contacts, and also have posted jobs with successful results. I like posting jobs on LinkedIn because it's cost-effective (costs less than half) compared to posting in the local [Atlanta] paper, and the candidates who reply to a posting on LinkedIn do so with built-in references."

Remember, you can search for jobs and get in touch with contacts at the companies where you would like to work directly on LinkedIn as well. Include the site on your list of job search sites to check regularly.

Kay Luo, former Director of Corporate Communications at LinkedIn, notes that

> LinkedIn's Advanced Search tool (under the People tab) is a real "gem" because of all the different ways to use it. For example, if you're not sure what your career track should be, you could do a keyword search on your existing/previous job title to see the profiles of other LinkedIn folks who had a similar position. Then you could see what their next jobs were, the companies they worked for, the skills they have, etc. All of this could guide you in your next move and how you might position yourself.

> Another way to use Advanced Search—If you landed an interview, see if the interviewer has a LinkedIn profile. Research their background to find out their job experience, as well as things you might have in common (same school, interests, positions).

> One more example—If there's a specific company you want to work for, enter it into the company search field and see whose profiles come up, and the degree of separation. Then leverage your close connections to get you that interview, even if it's just informational.

Niche Sites

There are niche jobs for just about every imaginable career field from jobs in advertising to jobs at the zoo. There are job sites, like Experience, that focus on college grads and entry-level positions, and job sites like CoolWorks (one of my personal favorites) that has all seasonal job listings.

One Day One Job (http://onedayonejob.com) focuses on entry-level positions for college graduates. At the other end of the career spectrum, RetiredBrains.com (http://www.retiredbrains.com) has full-time, part-time, and temporary retirement jobs for older workers.

If you're looking for a part-time job or an hourly job, there are sites dedicated to them. If you want to work for the government or in construction, you'll find sites with job listings. You can even find mystery shopper jobs online. There are sites focusing on those niches, as well.

Regardless of the level of job (from entry-level part-time to professional), you name it, there's a site for it. I have a directory of sites in various categories (http://tinyurl.com/2ee2sv) [jobsearch.about.com/od/jobsbycareerfieldaz/a/topsbytype.htm]. You can also search Google or Yahoo! by the type of job you are looking for (e.g., construction jobs or media jobs) to find niche job sites that match your career field of interest.

A word of warning—there are way too many sites that purport to have work-at-home job listings. Many of them are, at best, going to send you on a wild goose chase of a job hunt, and, at worst, take your money for nothing, or otherwise scam you. Be very careful before you apply for any work at home job, especially those that promise you lots of money for a little work. Check out the company and the job before you apply. I have detailed information on my About.com Job Searching site on avoiding work-at-home scams (http://tinyurl.com/nj2ro) [jobsearch.about.com/cs/workathomehelp/a/homescam.htm].

Social Networking Sites

Even though there are some job seekers who have found jobs on Facebook and Twitter, and the numbers will continue to increase, I wouldn't count on using social networking sites to find a job. Rather, they are tools that you should include in your job search arsenal, along with job boards, job search engines, LinkedIn, and other job search and networking sites.

Twitter

Twitter can help you find current job listings, get job search advice, and get information on careers, companies, and job opportunities. To avoid getting bogged down on Twitter, use tools to manage your Twitter feed.

Start by using a professional photo as your avatar and including a brief professional bio in your profile that highlights your experience. Include a link to your LinkedIn Profile or other online resume.

Twellow.com and MrTweet.com can help you find people to follow. Also, follow job sites and companies where you might like to work, so you'll get tweets with relevant employment information.

Facebook

Don't even think about job searching on Facebook until you have carefully set your privacy settings to ensure that hiring managers and business connections can only view what you want them to see.

Take a look at your photos. Are they appropriate for a hiring manager to see? How about the groups you belong to and your interests? If they aren't fit for public consumption, clean up your Facebook Profile before you use it to job search.

Then, take advantage of all the information on Facebook that can help you find a job. Most major job sites and companies have Facebook pages, some specifically for recruiting. There are Facebook apps geared to job searching, as well. To find Facebook job search apps, visit the Facebook Application Directory and search using "job search," "jobs," "career," or "employment" as keywords.

How to Job Search on Twitter and Facebook Videos

For more information on how to job search on Twitter and Facebook, take a look at these videos, which will step you through how to effectively use social networking sites.

- How to Job Search on Twitter (http://tinyurl.com/26kdvxc) [video.about.com/jobsearch/Job-Search-on-Twitter.htm]

- How to Job Search on Facebook (http://tinyurl.com/2asak7n) [video.about.com/jobsearch/Job-Search-Facebook.htm]

College Job Sites

Many college career offices provide job listings for alumni as well as students, partnering with sites like Experience.com and NACElink. Those job postings will be specifically for candidates from your alma mater. Check with your college career services or alumni offer to see if they have a job board you can access.

Job Searching Tips

You will find a variety of search options on the job sites. The best advice I can give you is to be specific and narrow your search using the Advanced Search options. The more specific your search, the better the results will match up with your skills and experience.

Narrowing your search will also enable you to reduce the number of job listings generated to an amount you can manage. Your goal is to find jobs that are worth applying to. Be sure you have the right qualifications for the jobs, and the jobs are the type of positions you want in the location where you want to work.

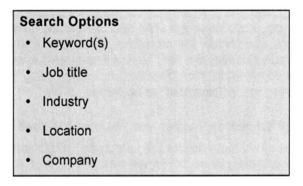

Search Options
- Keyword(s)
- Job title
- Industry
- Location
- Company

Advanced Search Options
- Radius of a location
- Job category
- Degree
- Posting date
- Salary range
- Company size or type

Keep Track

Remember that spreadsheet or job search management system you set up in Chapter 4? Now is when you're going to need it. Keep track of the jobs you applied for, the companies, where the jobs were posted and how (email, online, etc.), and when you applied. You may even want to copy and paste the job description into a Word document or an email message so you have a copy of what you applied for. That can be useful if you're contacted after the online listing has expired. Otherwise, you might not have a clue about what job you're interviewing for.

Use your tracking system as soon as you apply, or you're going to lose track of your applications. In some cases, you'll get email confirmation of your application. In others, your resume and letter might not be acknowledged.

The Numbers Game

Online job searching is a numbers game. There are almost too many job sites and you'll often find the same position posted on multiple sites. That's why it's important to keep track of your job search as it progresses.

On the flip side, the more applications you submit (as long as you're qualified) the greater the chance you have of getting interviews and the more chance you have of getting hired. So, apply for every job that is a match for your skills and interests. You'll probably end up having to juggle job offers at some point, but that's a good thing. It's better to have too many companies interested in you and job offers you can pick and choose from, than it is to have nothing in the hopper and no new job in sight.

RELATED RESOURCES

- Help Wanted Ads (http://tinyurl.com/2xle8e)
  [jobsearch.about.com/cs/nationwidejobs/a/helpwanted.htm]

- Job Listings (http://tinyurl.com/l9m85)
  [jobsearch.about.com/od/joblistings/qt/joblisting.htm]

- Job Search Engines (http://tinyurl.com/2f6yjg)
  [jobsearch.about.com/od/jobsearchengines/
  Job_Search_Engines.htm]

- Niche Job Sites (http://tinyurl.com/2ee2sv)
  [jobsearch.about.com/od/jobsbycareerfieldaz/a/
  topsbytype.htm]

6 Social Recruiting

Social Recruiting Overview

The advent of social media and the increase in utilization of social and professional networking sites like LinkedIn, Facebook, and Twitter, have changed the nature of how employers recruit. Companies are now going to where job seekers are to find candidates for employment.

Most companies have company pages on LinkedIn. When you visit a LinkedIn company page you'll see how you are connected to the company, open jobs, and insights into the company.

In addition, there's a Career tab for both companies and professionals. Job seekers can click on the tab to visit company pages to find out more about companies and about jobs at the company. You can also follow the company to stay abreast of the latest news and updates.

You'll also find company pages on Facebook especially designed to attract applicants. In addition to job listings, there is information on the company, on benefits, and the company culture. If you have a company you'd like to work for, search Facebook by company name to see if they have a Facebook page. If they do, you'll find a wealth of information that can help you apply and get selected for an interview at the company.

Companies are also using Twitter to tweet job postings, to tweet company news, and to attract candidates. Follow companies you'd like to work for to get the latest updates in your Twitter feed.

On all these sites, companies can discover more about you. For example, on Facebook, companies know who "likes" their page and companies know who is following them on Twitter. Making your presence known, by liking or following, can help you get noticed by a hiring manager or recruiter. Also, companies are interested in recruiting qualified candidates who show an interest in the company.

Then there are the sites designed for social recruiting. KODA.us includes facets of both Facebook and LinkedIn. After you sign up for KODA, you can add a photo, a video, and descriptive information about yourself, along with information from your resume.

KODA users can share videos, images, and links to blogs or other websites that showcase your background. In addition, personals profiles, employer profiles, and job opportunities can be shared on Facebook and Twitter.

Companies can post photos, videos, company information, and details on the hiring process for candidates, and can connect with job applicants via KODA's messaging system.

Talent Networks

As the integration between social media and recruiting continues, job boards are tapping into the power of social networking to engage job seekers.

CareerBuilder has launched a Talent Network which includes social media, personalized job recommendations, and employee referrals. The system also offers employers automated services to keep prospective applicants engaged with the company and to increase conversions from job listing viewers to applicants.

Dice has a social recruiting platform where job seekers can connect directly with recruiters. Job seekers can create profiles, which can include links to their social networking profiles, including LinkedIn, Facebook, YouTube, Twitter, and blogs.

In addition, job seekers can select which companies access their resumes and profiles, so they can maintain confidentiality while job searching. Companies and candidates can connect on Dice via a message center, real time chat, an instant message tool, and email.

Candidate Sourcing

Candidate sourcing includes other methods employers use to find candidates. They use LinkedIn, alumni associations, professional associations, directories like Hoovers.com, and referrals; and they even simply search Google to find strong applicants for employment.

Employers are also using candidate sourcing programs that are designed to find applicants. Airs Sourcepoint, for example, is used by many Fortune 500 companies, and it searches multiple databases for candidates who match the company's specifications.

Power Resume Search enables employers to search Monster's resume database by keyword, location, education, employer, job title, and skills. It also searches by when the resume was updated, so keeping your resume current makes good sense.

Using systems like these, hiring managers can then contact candidates quickly and simply.

Company Hiring Consortiums

Companies are creating consortiums to gather their own pools of applicants. AllianceQ, for example, is made up of a group of Fortune 500 companies that have collaborated to create a pool of job applicants. Job seekers who register with AllianceQ can be found, confidentially, by leading companies. After you register, you create an online resume and select your career interests. Then, if you are of interest to the companies that are hiring, you receive invitations to apply for jobs from the companies that are interested in talking to you.

JobCentral is another employer managed job site. You'll find job listings from over 500 top member companies; you can search or browse the job listings; and you can upload your resume to apply.

These types of sites are a way for job seekers to get directly to employers with current available job openings and a way to connect with leading employers who may not advertise jobs elsewhere.

Social Recruiting and Your Career

What's most important about social recruiting, and I think we've only seen the start of how it's going to evolve, is that companies are everywhere you are.

That can be a disadvantage if you're not careful about what you post online. On the flip side, it can be a huge advantage when it comes to job searching. The more venues companies are using for recruiting, the more opportunities you have to find job leads and the more opportunities to make connections.

Just as importantly, the more chances you will have to be found by recruiters and hiring managers who are seeking candidates with your skills and experience.

RELATED RESOURCES

- Social Recruiting and Your Job Search
  (http://tinyurl.com/cb73mg)
  [jobsearch.about.com/od/onlinecareernetworking/a/
  socialrecruiting.htm]

- Top Social Networking Sites for Job Search
  (http://tinyurl.com/csowpc)
  [jobsearch.about.com/od/networkingsites/a/
  networkingsites.htm]

- Job Searching Where Companies Can Find You
  (http://tinyurl.com/lg3zh6)
  [jobsearch.about.com/od/companyresearch/a/
  companyhiring.htm]

7 Active vs. Passive Job Seeking

Passive and Active Job Seeking Overview

What's the difference between seeking a job actively and seeking a job passively? An active job seeker is someone who needs to find a job *now*. Active job seekers could be out of work or about to lose their job, or they hate their job, or the pay isn't enough, or the schedule doesn't work. When you're actively job seeking, finding a new job sooner rather than later is essential.

Passive job seeking is different. You are a passive job seeker when you don't really need to find a new job, but you would consider the right opportunity if it presented itself. Most of us are, or should be, passive job seekers—all the time.

Anyone who is on any type of career track should be, at least, passively marketing themself. If you're just starting out your career, being ready to move on will help you move up the career ladder. Mid-career professionals can be well positioned to consider job offers that will boost their career. Career changers can get well situated to make a change, and those considering retirement options can prepare for whatever is next on the horizon.

In addition, you never know when you might lose your job, so it's important to be prepared to switch from passive to active job seeking mode. One company I worked for eliminated my job and everyone else's job nationwide in the same position. They simply eliminated a layer of management to save money. We went to work one morning, that same afternoon we had six weeks of severance pay, an unemployment slip (this was in the days of paper), and we had turned in our company car and company credit card.

That can happen to any one of us. Regardless of how secure you think your job is, none of us are indispensable or irreplaceable, despite how much we might think the company values us. Getting fired or laid off can happen to the best of us. That's why it's important to be prepared for any eventuality and to consider opportunities that may help us get where we can go, from a career (and life) perspective as we find them,—or they find us.

How Hiring Managers and Recruiters Seek Passive Candidates

Not all companies advertise job openings online. In fact, many companies look for referrals as a first choice for finding new employees. That's why you'll see hiring bonuses (of hundreds or even thousands of dollars) offered to current employees who refer candidates that are hired by their company. The logic is that a candidate who comes highly recommended will most likely be a better hire than a random person who submitted a resume.

Referrals aren't the only way companies hire new employees. You will, of course, find many (too many in some cases) job listings on the Internet, but there are a variety of other sources employers utilize.

Tom Chambers, Executive Search Recruiter at firstPRO, says, "Everyone in this business has a different method, but the one thing you will hear most say is to use the 'who do you know' line with everyone. Other methods I use a lot are Google, state professional license databases (i.e., CPA, engineer, doctor, etc.), and LinkedIn has been helpful in the past. Hoovers and alumni websites are also useful."

Andrea Santiago, Healthcare Recruiter and Health Careers Guide for About.com explains, "Large national recruiting firms typically have research tools which would help find passive candidates, particularly for high-level and management positions. These tools such as Hoovers.com, Lexis-Nexis, and OneSource.com allow users to research our client's competing firms, and then pull up a list of managers at each of those firms, which we could then call with a name already in hand!"

Andrea adds, "There are times when we would possibly turn to professional association websites to access names, and in those instances, a candidate would obviously have to be a member of the association in order to be found by us recruiters."

Technical Recruiter Marcus Ronaldi notes that recruiting doesn't all happen online. "Going to a trade show or conference, networking event or user group is an offline way of finding passive candidates."

Michael Rocha, Recruiting Consultant at Davron Staffing, suggests getting involved as a way to increase your exposure, suggesting job seekers can:

1. Write for a specialized publication, local newspaper, city newspaper, flyer, etc. Once you do this, you can upload to a blog and submit it to several sources.
2. Publish a YouTube video about your area of specialization.
3. Join LinkedIn.
4. Volunteer.

College alumni associations are another good source of candidates for employment. Most colleges have a strong alumni community who are eager to recruit other alumni from the institution. In many cases, the Career Services office is among the first places that alumni use to list an opening or seek candidates.

Use Passive Job Seeking to Your Advantage

Why does it make sense to be prepared for a job search? Besides being ready if you're in the position of having to find a job, you will also be in a position to react immediately if someone comes along and offers you the job of your dreams. You won't have to scramble to update your resume that's ten years out-of-date or pull together something to wear to meet the person who might be your next boss.

Here's how to be a proactive passive job seeker:

- **Have a current resume.** Update it whenever you find a new job or get a promotion.

- **Update your profiles.** When you change jobs, update your Facebook, LinkedIn, and other profiles. Update with new email addresses, phone numbers, etc., as well. Make sure your profiles are fully completed with all relevant information.

- **Join in.** Join your college alumni association and join professional associations related to your career field. Remember, these are places recruiters look for candidates.

- **Keep in touch.** Keep in touch with your contacts, even if it's just to see how they are doing.

- **Have references ready.** Have a list of contacts and previous managers who have already agreed to give you a reference.

- **Notify colleges and associations.** Again, when your job changes, send a quick note to let your alma mater and your professional associations know about the change.

- **Keep up your skills.** Technology often seems to change faster than the speed of light, so be sure to keep your skills up-to-date and stay on top of new technologies and tools.

- **Know your industry.** Stay current as well with what's happening in your career field and industry. It's important to be knowledgeable and informed.

Knowing your industry is important. Even though it can be hard to keep up with what's happening, from a career perspective, it's very valuable—and an asset to your future employers to be aware of trends and changes in your industry.

It's not always easy to stay on top of what's new and noteworthy, but it is worthwhile. For example, when I started writing about job searching for About.com (then the Mining Co.) over twelve years ago (which is almost a lifetime in Internet time), jobs were posted on job banks and you had to visit each one to search for job listings and apply. In many cases, you had to mail a paper resume and cover letter to apply.

To date myself even further, I remember when we got job postings from JobTrak (later to become MonsterTrak) by fax. We had those listings in binders and recorded other listings on a telephone job line for job seekers to access. There weren't any databases for jobs and internships, as there are now.

Since then, we have had more changes than I can easily keep track of—job search engines, social and professional networking, niche job sites, resume zapping services, instant message and cell phone applications for job seekers, online application systems, point and click uploads of resumes and cover letters, video interviewing, etc. It's gotten much easier to find jobs, apply, and interview. On the other hand, there are a lot more resources to figure out what to do with.

If I hadn't stayed current with what was happening in the world of jobs and careers, I would have most likely been out of business a long time ago. It's my job to stay current, but it's valuable for all of us to do the same.

TIPS FOR STAYING CURRENT

- *Set up Google alerts* for your industry and/or career field, and for companies you are interested in. Google will send you an email to let you know when there is new information available online.

- *Skim the newspaper daily* and read at least one news magazine each week.

- *Read books* (reading really isn't a lost art). I get a lot of reading done when I travel—it's a good time to set aside for the stack of books I need to get through.
- *Take a class.* Especially if you're a person in high-tech, take a class or a workshop to keep your skills up.
- *Try a tool.* If you haven't tried instant messaging, give it a shot. Not sure about networking sites? Give them a try too. If you hear about something new, check it out—someone told me about Jott.com this morning (you can send email reminders to yourself by phone), so I went to the site to see if it could be helpful.
- *Attend conferences.* Attend industry and trade conferences and seminars. You'll not only learn what's new in your field, you will be able to make connections as well.

So, what's the benefit of what probably seems like work? There is one really big benefit besides being ready if you lose your job—you'll also be ready if you get that call from a contact about your dream job. If a hiring manager, a recruiter, or a contact gets in touch with you and asks if you would be interested in a new opportunity, you'll be ready.

You will have a resume ready to send (immediately) and you'll be able to make a bottom-line decision based on the job, not on how long it would take you to pull together the credentials you need to apply. You will be able to decide if the job is worth considering (the job, the salary, the benefits, the location, the level of the job, etc., are all a good fit) or not. You can do that based on the job, not based on how much you would have to scramble.

Having to scramble can cost you the opportunity. Dahlia, for example, had been working for the same company for quite a few years. She had a good job and was satisfied with it. She got a call from a recruiter who advised her that a competitor was recruiting candidates for an upper management job, which would be a few steps up the career ladder for her, and wanted to talk to her.

Given that she wasn't planning to job search, her resume was ancient and Dahlia spent too long tweaking it. By the time she got it updated, it was too late. They had moved on to other candidates.

Keep in mind, as well, that you don't have to take a job or even go on an interview if you're not interested in the position. Declining is fine, just do it diplomatically so you can use the contact in the future, if need be. The goal is to be in a position to be able to say, "Yes, I'm interested," or "No, thank you," without having to think about anything other than the job at hand.

How to Ensure Employers Find You

Your goal, even if you aren't seeking a job today, is to be in a position where employers can find you if they have a job you're qualified for. Build that professional brand we spoke about in Chapter 1 and build an online presence. I've spoken to recruiters who have found candidates just by Googling the qualifications they are looking for. Your presence online will help market you as a strong candidate for a company to consider. And, after all, every employer wants to hire the best and the brightest.

Executive Recruiter Tom Chambers suggests:

1. Unless you are desperate to make an immediate change, do not post a public resume. Get indirect information out there. Create a LinkedIn account, blog, etc. You want to come up on a Google search.

2. Find one or two good recruiters with direct experience working searches with your skill set and with companies you would be interested in. Keep the number of recruiters low, because it doesn't look good to a hiring authority if multiple recruiters call them about one person.

How to Get Jobs to Come to You

Being in a position where you can easily be found is one way to passively job search. However, you also might want to be in a position where you can view job listings that might be of interest, even if you're not actively seeking employment.

Given the online job searching technology that's available, it's quick and easy to get the jobs to come to you. It only takes a few minutes to set up job search alerts so you can receive notifications of new listings that match the search criteria you set, or to tweak your profiles to let contacts know you might be interested in career opportunities. You can even get new job postings via text message. Collegegrad.com, for example, is one of the websites that will send targeted text or video cell phone messages from an employer to a target audience.

Set Up Job Alerts and Notifications

- Set up job search agents to receive new posting notifications via email.

- Build your network and manage your connections, so they are available when you might need them.

- Check company sites. If you have a company on your "wish list" that you'd like to work for, check its website frequently for new job listings.

- Edit your contact settings. Make sure you have the following options selected in your LinkedIn contact settings so everyone will know your availability:

  - career opportunities

  - job inquiries

  - expertise requests

  - business deals

  - reference requests

  - getting back in touch

Another option is to go online every once in a while to see what's out there. Use the job search engines to run a quick search for the type and number of jobs available in your field. Also, use one of the salary sites (like PayScale.com or salary.com) to see what you're worth. Being informed is one of the best job search tools you can have.

Build Bridges, Don't Burn Them

One of the other best job search tools you can have is manners. Be polite if you decline a job or if you leave your job. You never know when you might need a reference or if the company who turned you down might have a more appropriate opening in the future.

I won't forget the student who had applied for an internship. She received a polite email from a human resources manager expressing regret at not being able to hire her for a summer position. She wrote back to the HR manager and said, "Your loss." That was it, but, besides being rude, it was enough to cost her any chance of future employment at that firm.

I have had, and still have, a good relationship with every one of my employers. Despite the fact that I moved on, I did it diplomatically, by providing two weeks notice and offering to help with the transition. I also stayed in touch with my connections, so I can, if need be, get a reference, even years after I worked for the company.

Staying in touch whenever possible, with clients and coworkers, also makes good sense. The more connections you have, the better positioned you will be to get a new job, whenever you need one. That way, the jobs really will be coming to you, and you won't have worked hard to make it happen.

RELATED RESOURCES

- How to Say Goodbye (http://tinyurl.com/yvmx9s) [jobsearch.about.com/od/resignation/a/saygoodbye.htm]

- Job Search Engines (http://tinyurl.com/2f6yjg) [jobsearch.about.com/od/jobsearchengines/ Job_Search_Engines.htm]

- Salary Calculators (http://tinyurl.com/32om26) [jobsearch.about.com/od/salarysurveys/a/ salarysurveys.htm]

8 Online Job Search Management Tools

How do you keep track of your job search? What do you do with copies of resumes and cover letters you have sent and email you need to follow up on? How about scheduling interviews and making phone calls?

When you're actively job seeking, keeping track and getting organized can be really confusing. So, it makes sense to organize your job search activities, and then keep the system you have established in place as your career grows and transitions.

Once you have a system in place, filing, following up, scheduling, etc., will become routine rather than scattered activities that you, if you're anything like I am, will be stressing over.

It makes it much easier when you can be reminded (electronically or otherwise) that you need to follow up on a resume you sent or send a thank you note after an interview. There are free tools that you can use to effectively manage your job search. Start using some of them and you'll save yourself a ton of time.

Once you get set up, you will be able to manage your entire job search from any computer, regardless of where you are. Here's what you will be able to accomplish:

1. Email—online access to your email
2. Documents—online access to your resume, cover letter, and other job search documents
3. Calendar—schedule interviews and appointments via the web
4. Task Management—manage all your job searching activities online

JibberJobber

Jason Alba, CEO of JibberJobber.com, founded the company when he was job searching. He realized that there weren't any good tools available for managing his job search. He saw the need for a better job search management system and created exactly that. Jason explains the benefits of JibberJobber saying, "JibberJobber replaces spreadsheets, notebooks, and file folders and allows you to organize everything surrounding current and future job searches, all in one place. You save time (since you don't have to create your own system) and stress, with the peace of mind knowing that you'll have all of your appointments and job search intelligence in one place. Since the information never goes away, your database grows in value with each new job search, or as you network more, which will help in subsequent job searches or promotions."

JibberJobber does more than just manage your job search, even though it's very good at that. You can use it to manage your entire career. JibberJobber is web based, so you can keep track of all your information online. You will know where you have sent resumes, which jobs you have applied for, as well as where you are in the hiring process.

Users can track their networking contacts and keep a log of how they have helped, as well as get in touch with them via LinkedIn, right from within JibberJobber.

JibberJobber is a terrific tool for managing job search information, as well as getting and staying organized. It's easily accessible online and simple to use. The basic version is free and the premium version has some added bells and whistles that are worth the investment.

Online Job Search Management

Other tools you can get to help expedite your job search include widgets that post new jobs on your MySpace, Facebook, computer or Google desktop, toolbar, or blog. Other options include buttons and plug-ins for your browsers, RSS feeds, and instant message and email alerts. The job search engines, Indeed and SimplyHired, for example, both have a full selection of tools you can install.

Paul Forster, CEO of Indeed.com, says, "One of the best ways to manage your online job searches is by saving your searches and having jobs emailed to you." By setting up a my.indeed account, you may also save individual jobs, add notes to saved job listings, and manage your email job alerts. User accounts are great for organizing and keeping track of all your online job search activities.

Email Options

Microsoft Outlook

I use email to keep track of a lot of items on my "to do" list. I have folders set up for various activities and I use them to organize and file my correspondence, most of which is via email these days. It's useful to set up a folder for Resumes Sent and to bcc (blind carbon copy) yourself every time you email a resume. That way, you can keep a copy of what you have sent in an email file.

I also have a Follow Up folder where I keep track of the people I need to reply to and the emails I've sent that I need to follow up on.

There are different options for email. Microsoft Outlook is a computer-based email system, so once you have downloaded your email to your computer you won't be able to access it from the web. It does, however, have an Address Book where you can keep track of your contacts and a Calendar to keep track of your daily activities. I don't go anywhere without my laptop, so I use Outlook for most of the emailing I do.

That said, I do have web access to all my email accounts so I can access them from anywhere I have Internet access.

Web-Based Email

You may, or may not, be surprised to know that most people job search from work. They look for jobs during the day, on company time, rather than on evenings and weekends. I won't get into the ethics of job shopping on company time, but if you're one of those people, you should consider using a web email application.

First of all, you definitely shouldn't be using your company computer (and email client) for job searching. Some companies monitor email activity, so job searching on company time could cost you the job you currently have. It's also a really bad idea to send email using your work email address. A prospective new employer won't be impressed that you're using your present company's email server to look for work.

The simple solution is to use web-based email. That way you can check email frequently and respond to job search communications in a timely manner. From what I hear, don't use an AOL email address if you're looking for a tech job (some say for any job), it's not cool—or professional. Gmail (Google's online email service) or Yahoo! are more acceptable in the eyes of professionals and hiring managers.

Calendars

Once you've started applying for jobs, employers will start contacting you to schedule interviews. Interviews can either be in person, on the phone, or even via video. You may be contacted by email or by phone. In either case, you need to be prepared to schedule interviews.

If you're working, try to schedule interviews for early or late in the day, or even at lunchtime. Otherwise, if you need to take time off to interview, you could schedule a couple of interviews on the same day (leaving plenty of time between interviews for travel) and take a personal day from work.

It's essential to keep track of your interviews (and when you need to follow up with your connections). So, you'll need a calendar program of one sort or another to manage your schedule.

Calendar Options

- Daily/weekly planner

- PDA (personal digital assistant)

- Outlook Calendar

- Free online calendars such as Google or Yahoo!

- Web-based or computer-based calendar programs

If you use Microsoft Outlook as your email client, you can use the built-in calendar. There are daily, weekly, and monthly views, and there is an option to set reminders so you don't miss important events. You can also use the Tasks section to create a "to do" list. Both your calendar and your tasks will show in the right sidebar of your email, so you will see what you need to do when you're in the program.

Online calendars are typically integrated or linked from your online email account and your contacts. Yahoo!, for example, in addition to your mail, shows your calendar, your Yahoo! messenger contacts, and has a notepad for jotting down reminders and other notes. When you're in Gmail, you will see links to your calendar and your documents.

Documents

When you're not in a position to sit at home all day sending out resumes, it makes sense to have your documents online where you can access them from anywhere. That way, if you need to send a resume sooner rather than later, you won't have to wait until you get home.

Google Docs is easy (and free) to use. You can upload documents directly from your computer (browse to select the file, then click to upload) or create a new document right on the website. You can edit your documents (which is perfect for cover letter writing) and export them as Word, OpenOffice, PDF, RTF, or HTML files.

Microsoft Office users can use Microsoft Office Live Workspace, which is also free, to save and access up to 1000 documents online. You can save your resumes, letters, and other documents online, plus you can organize projects (your job search), add notes, and create a list of tasks you need to do.

There are also programs, like GoToMyPC.com, where you can access the files on your computer from any web browser or wireless device.

Backup Copies

I've lost, more than once, important files on my computer because I hadn't backed them up in a timely manner. So, do make sure you have backup copies of your resume and other job searching documents. You can save a copy online, back up your entire system online or to an external hard drive, or save copies of your most important documents on a CD.

Remember, in the long run, it's much more work to try and recreate what you've lost if your computer crashes than it is to take a few minutes to make sure everything important is backed up somewhere.

More Tools

There is, of course, the old-fashioned way of keeping organized and keeping track. I probably shouldn't admit it, but sometimes I'm a paper person. I have a couple of "to do" lists; one for items that need immediate attention, and the other for longer-term projects. I have a wall calendar that keeps track of appointments, a desktop planner, and a weekly planner that goes everywhere I go.

To take it one step further, I know one couple who use a color-coded wall calendar. He has a color, she has a color, and they have a third color for joint activities. That way, they can see at a glance who is supposed to be where, and when.

An alternative is to set up a simple Excel spreadsheet. Include companies you have applied to, contacts, email addresses and phone numbers, and some columns for dates and follow-up activity.

When you are applying for jobs that require online applications (like retail or temporary positions), rather than submitting a resume, the quickest and easiest way to keep track is just to keep a list of where and when you applied. Jot down your user name and password if you had to create an account, then make a note to check on the status of your application.

Another timesaving tip is to "just do it." I could have saved hours if I had just done the task that I spent time adding to my "to do" list. If it's something quick and simple and only takes a couple of minutes to do, it can make better sense to do it and forget about it, rather than tracking it.

The bottom line is that there isn't a right or wrong system to get (and stay) organized. Whatever works for you is absolutely fine to use. The key is to have a system of one kind or another. The last thing you want to do is miss an interview or not follow up because you forgot. When it comes to getting hired, forgetting isn't an acceptable excuse. The only thing you can forget, probably, is getting a job offer.

It doesn't matter how you get organized. What's important is that you are organized in a way that works for you. Regardless of which method(s) you choose, figure out a way to keep track of all your job search and career building activities. It will make the process much simpler and smoother, and it makes your life easier, as well.

RELATED RESOURCES

- Google Docs (http://docs.google.com)

- JibberJobber (http://jibberjobber.com)

- Job Search Toolkit (http://tinyurl.com/365o7e)
  [jobsearch.about.com/od/jobsearchtips/a/jobsearchtool.htm]

- Microsoft Office Live Workspace
  (http://workspace.officelive.com/)

- Online Calendars (http://tinyurl.com/37qznt)
  [websearch.about.com/od/dailywebsearchtips/qt/
  dnt0424.htm]

- Online Word Processing Software (http://tinyurl.com/ypllad)
  [wordprocessing.about.com/od/choosingsoftware/Choosing
  _a_Word_Processor_That_Suits_Your_Needs.htm]

- Top Free Email Services (http://tinyurl.com/2xw74d)
  [email.about.com/od/freeemailreviews/tp/free_email.htm]

---

9 Online Communications

If your mom is anything like mine, she spent a good amount of time while you were growing up telling you that how you say something is as important as what you say. Sometimes, and I don't like to admit it very often, our mothers are right. All your communications need to be polished and professional.

When I get an email that says, "can u help me fnd job plz," instead of, "Could you please help me find a job?" and continues without proper spelling, paragraph spacing, or punctuation, my tendency is to ignore it. Sometimes, it is hard just trying to figure out the question. There is even an online slang translator available (http://www.noslang.com), but if I have to work that hard to decipher the message, I'm probably not going to bother.

The Simple Solution

There's a simple solution: don't do it. When you're applying for a job or asking for job search help, use proper language, not acronyms or Internet slang. That's any job, by the way. If you're filling out an online application for a job at Walmart or Home Depot or wherever, make sure your application is grammatically correct and without typos. If you're not sure, ask someone to proof it for you before hitting the "submit" button. As an aside, so you don't think I'm picking on certain types of candidates, I've received worse letters (with awful misspellings and typos) from college graduates and Master's level candidates than I have for some janitorial positions.

Speaking of jobs, I did hire someone once who couldn't read and write too well, but Sam Jones was smart. He had his wife fill out his application for him and it was perfect. She also took care of the new-hire paperwork. The job he was applying for didn't require reading or writing, so it didn't really matter and Sam was one of the best employees I had ever hired. He never missed a day of work and he had lots of suggestions that saved our company significant amounts of money. He was our Employee of the Year one year, and the trip to our company retreat, where he was awarded the honor, was his first trip (and Sam was close to retirement) out of the small town where he had lived his entire life.

Sam was an exception, though. For the most part, employers want literate employees who can string a sentence together without glaring grammatical errors. The trick when communicating online, whether it's via email, instant message, Facebook, or LinkedIn messaging, is to write as though you were writing a perfect letter on paper. Spell check, grammar check, proofread, reread your message, and, again, ask someone to proof it for you, if you're not sure it's perfect.

Reading what you wrote out loud is another good tip for picking up mistakes. It isn't so easy to find mistakes, but reading your message will help you discover missing words or grammatically incorrect sentences.

Perfect Communication Do's and Don'ts

- **Do** reread your messages and check for typos and grammatical errors before you send them.

- **Don't** use acronyms, abbreviations, or slang.

- **Do** address people you don't know formally as Ms. or Mr. rather than by first name.

- **Do** write messages with full sentences and paragraphs.

- **Do** explain (in the first paragraph) who you are and why you are writing when contacting people who don't know you.

Email

When you are sending email, it's important to keep your message short and to the point. I've read that people don't often read beyond the first paragraph so you need to capture their attention within the first few sentences. Your emails, just like your other correspondence, need to be grammatically correct and not have any typos.

Most people are deluged with email. It's hard to manage when you get a very high volume of email and anyone who makes your life easier by following proper email protocol will be appreciated.

TIPS FOR EMAIL COMMUNICATION

- **Subject line:** If you're applying for a job, put your name and the job title you're applying for in the subject line of your email message. If you're writing to a contact, describe what you're writing about, e.g., Career Advice Request or Job Search Assistance. Never send a message with a blank subject line. It probably won't get opened.

- **Signature:** Each message should include your signature. Your signature should include your full name, your email address, and links to your websites, if you have them.

- **Message Content:** Keep the body of your message to a couple of paragraphs of a few sentences each. Your message needs to be focused and targeted, so the reader knows at a glance why you are writing. Proofread and spell check your message prior to sending it.

- **Return Receipt:** Turn it off. Hiring managers and others helping with your job search don't want to have to prove they read your message. I automatically say "no" any time I get one.

- **Spam Blocker:** Turn it off. Employers and contacts don't want to have to go online to verify who they are in order to read your message.

- **Wait to Follow Up:** Don't send a message a few hours or even a day after your first one, asking if the person received it. Be patient and give them time to respond.

Instant Message (IM)

Instant messaging can help with your job search. If you have an instant message account, you can use it for networking with your IM buddies and with professional contacts who have instant message accounts. Be forewarned, though, not to talk about your job search the same way you talk to your buddies about your personal life. You will need to have a presentable screen name and you will need to write messages using professional language, full words, and sentences rather than acronyms and sentence fragments.

Instant messaging can be helpful because it's another networking tool. People can't help you with job searching if they don't know you're looking for a job. So, if you mention it to your buddies, they may be able to assist.

Also, you may be able to get job search assistance via instant message. For example, some college career service offices and private counselors provide distance counseling via instant message and email.

There are applications, like Digsby, you can use to manage all your IM, email, and social networking accounts from one place. It's a free download and it can save some time managing multiple accounts.

Instant Messenger Services

- AOL Instant Messenger (AIM)

- Digsby

- Google Talk

- Trillian

- Windows Live Messenger

- Yahoo! Messenger

Networking Site Messaging

When you're messaging via a networking site, the same rules apply. Anything related to your job search needs to be professional and proof-read. Again, be descriptive of what you want if you don't know the person you're writing to, and if you're asking for help, be clear as to what assistance you're looking for, and, of course, be polite.

Be selective. Don't send a blast message to everyone you know asking for help. Send individual messages tailored to the recipient. You'll get a better response if you write individually and ask for personalized assistance.

Video Resumes, Profiles, and Interviewing

A video resume can boost your career or make your career come to a screeching halt. It depends. You may have heard the story of the now infamous college senior who sent around a video showing himself playing tennis and ballroom dancing. That didn't help his prospects. On the other end of the spectrum, well-done video resumes have helped job seekers secure an interview.

I've seen some pretty awful video resumes and some good ones. If you search YouTube for "resume" or "video resume," you can get some ideas of what you should do if you create one, and what you shouldn't do. My advice is not to do it unless you're in a career field where it will be of interest to employers and not to do it unless you can do it professionally.

Susan Heathfield, About.com's Human Resources Guide, shares the employer's perspective on video resumes:

> Vault.com's annual survey of employers found that 83% of employers are willing to look at a video resume, but they have concerns. First, they can use the video resume to assess your professionalism and presentation. But, the ones they've seen so far have hurt the candidate most frequently because they've been made unprofessionally.
>
> Then, some employers are worried that the video resume will result in claims of discrimination from candidates who were not hired. Employment law attorneys are split on the issue of video resumes, with many advising employers not to accept them. Their main concern about video resumes is that they provide information about an applicant's race, sex, disability, and age, all details that could become part of a discrimination lawsuit.
>
> But, my biggest concern, as an employer, is the amount of time I would need to invest in watching them. I can read a resume for pertinent qualifications in thirty seconds, without worrying about unfairly discriminating; the video takes much longer. So, I'd prefer to receive old fashioned resumes and cover letters unless the position requires presentation skills.

So, before taking the time to make a video resume, decide if it's worth the effort and how much it will help your job search. If you decide to give it a try, review these tips before you start recording.

Video Resume Do's and Don'ts

- **Don't** make a video resume unless you can do it well.

- Write a script. That way you're not rambling away and your video is focused.

- **Do** dress in professional business attire.

- **Don't** have a busy background; a plain wall works much better than your messy home office or living room.

- **Do** look at the video camera, not at the desk or table below you.

- **Don't** speak too fast or too slow.

- **Do** begin the video by mentioning your name, and then give a brief description of your skills and experience.

- **Don't** discuss your personal life—this is a professional marketing pitch, not a personal one.

- **Do** discuss the value you would offer to a potential employer.

If you do create a video resume that you're proud of, show it to some acquaintances to be sure that they see it the same way. If it adds value (and that's the key point) to your candidacy for employment, list it on your paper/online resume, add a link to it from your website or blog, and consider posting it online. In addition to YouTube, there are job search sites like CareerBuilder, Jobster, Monster India, and MyWorkster where you can upload your video resume.

Video Interview Tips

Video interviewing is very different from video resumes. A video interview is a long distance interview that takes place via video instead of in person. Video interviewing saves employers time and money, especially when hiring long-distance candidates. The other employer benefit is consistency. Each candidate can be asked the same set of questions and their responses can be compared. It also saves the interviewer from having to remember which candidate said what.

Mark Newman, CEO of HireVue, shared his tips for successful video interviewing:

- Dress the same way you would for an in-person interview—in professional attire.

- Review the instructions. Request assistance if you're not sure how the webcam works or if you have questions. You should be able to get help online or over the phone.

- Follow the directions. The process will run smoothly if you follow the step-by-step directions.

- Practice interviewing. Record yourself if you have a video camera or webcam, so you can see how you look on camera.

- Look straight at the camera—don't look around the room or down at the desk.

- Sit back, relax, and tell a story—the video interview is used to get to know you better.

Michael Policano, CEO/Founder of LiveHire, another video interviewing service, adds, "There are many benefits of using video interviewing for both employers and candidates. Immediately there are savings in cost and time. For employers that do a lot of college recruiting, they will be able to interview college graduates without restriction of travel, time, and money, hence opening the opportunity to many more schools than a recruiter could travel to. Candidates who are far away in another state or even country will be given the same consideration as local candidates, giving them more opportunity to choose the right company. Employers would not think twice about flying a candidate in to meet face-to-face after they already met online. It's the next best thing to being in the same room as the interviewer."

For the candidate, video interviewing can save travel time and expense. Being in front of a camera can be a little nerve wracking, especially for some of us, but the video interviewing company will help you with the process and the equipment. So, be sure to ask if you have any questions.

Prepare for a video interview the same way you do for in-person interviews. Research the company so you are prepared to answer questions. Dress the same way, too. The only difference between a video interview and an in-office interview is that you're not sitting face to face with the interviewer. How you present yourself and how your candidacy is evaluated works exactly the same way.

The Benefits of Effective Communication

Communicating well is what is going to make the best impression on a potential employer. A poorly written cover letter or resume, or an email riddled with typos, isn't going to get you anywhere. What you do wrong is noticed more often than what you do right.

There is so much competition for every available job that the candidates who don't present themselves and communicate well knock themselves out of contention before they even get a chance to set foot inside an interview room. Employers want literate employees with excellent communication skills, because those employees represent the company to the outside world.

Writing perfect correspondence may not get you the job, but it will certainly get your application materials considered—and that's the first step in the hiring process.

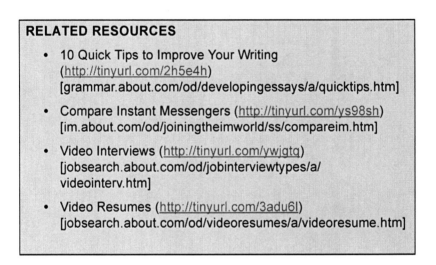

RELATED RESOURCES

- 10 Quick Tips to Improve Your Writing (http://tinyurl.com/2h5e4h) [grammar.about.com/od/developingessays/a/quicktips.htm]

- Compare Instant Messengers (http://tinyurl.com/ys98sh) [im.about.com/od/joiningtheimworld/ss/compareim.htm]

- Video Interviews (http://tinyurl.com/ywjgtq) [jobsearch.about.com/od/jobinterviewtypes/a/videointerv.htm]

- Video Resumes (http://tinyurl.com/3adu6l) [jobsearch.about.com/od/videoresumes/a/videoresume.htm]

Chapter 9: Online Communications

10 Job Search Apps

Job Search Apps Overview

How job seekers look for jobs has certainly changed over the years. When job searching first moved online, the only way to job hunt online was through a job board where companies posted open positions. Newspapers added online job postings. Companies started listing jobs on their corporate websites. Then the job search engines made it easy to search multiple job sites with a few clicks.

Now, you can search for jobs, apply for jobs, and manage your job applications right from your phone or iPad. Monster, for example, has an iPad app where job seekers can search for jobs, sign into their Monster account, save searches, get email alerts when new jobs are posted, save jobs, apply for jobs, and check to see what jobs they have applied for.

That's just one of many apps available that enables job seekers to search for jobs from anywhere. In addition to phone and iPad apps there are Facebook apps available that allow job seekers to tap into their network of friends to job search and for career networking.

iPhone and iPad Apps

There are plenty of apps available for job searching and networking. Many apps are free, others cost a few dollars. Before you spend money on an app, consider whether it's worth it, or whether you could get the same information elsewhere free.

As I mentioned, job seekers are able to access their Monster account information to search or and apply to jobs via their iPad. The application includes the ability to use the built-in GPS to search for jobs near where you're located, enabling a quick view into the most relevant jobs close to home.

Another useful app is professional networking site LinkedIn's app. LinkedIn users cans bring along their professional network with them wherever they go. Users have immediate access to their LinkedIn invitations, connections, messages, and network updates such as when someone in their network posts a lead for a new open position. If you have Bluetooth enabled on your iPhone you can connect instantly with other LinkedIn users who are close by.

When you want to find job listings, use the LinkUp Job Search Engine app to search for jobs on company websites by keyword, location, company, and category. Users can save jobs to your Favorites and access them via a web browser or RSS feed reader. Searches can be saved and you can apply to jobs through your iPhone and/or email job openings to yourself (or a friend) so you can apply at your convenience.

There are just a few of the apps that are available. You'll find more listed on the About.com Job Search site list of apps (http://tinyurl.com/5stfngs) [jobsearch.about.com/od/jobsearchapps/apps-for-job-searching.htm]. You can also visit Apple's iTunes store to find more apps to help you job search.

How to Find Job Search Apps

If you know what app you want to install, visit the App Store on your iPhone or iPad by tapping on the icon on your phone and search for the application you are interested in. Or, visit Apple's online App Store or your iTune account.

Facebook Apps

The lines between work and play, and business and pleasure, continue to blur—if there are any left. The interaction between websites and Facebook is also becoming more seamless.

You can add job alerts or job search widgets to your Facebook page. SimplyHired's "Who Do I Know?" tool lets you see who you know on Facebook and LinkedIn when you search for jobs on SimplyHired.

Indeed also has tools for networking, including a Facebook widget that helps you find jobs where your friends work and lets you use Indeed to search from your Facebook page.

BranchOut is a Facebook app designed specifically for career networking. Your LinkedIn profile can be imported to BranchOut, so you will have a professional profile on Facebook. You can browse your friends on Facebook to see where they have worked and you can view open positions at their company. You can browse and share jobs that people within your career network have posted and you can give and get BranchOut endorsements.

If you use CareerBuilder's Facebook app, you can have updated job and internship postings delivered directly from CareerBuilder to your Facebook profile. CareerBuilder uses your location and career interests to send you relevant job profiles. You can then follow a link directly from the job listing to apply for the job online.

How to Find Facebook Job Search Apps

To find employment-related Facebook apps, login to Facebook, click on Profile, type the application name in the search box, then follow the instructions to install. Or, visit the Facebook Application Directory and search using "job search," "career," "employment," or "jobs" as keywords.

Facebook Apps and Privacy

It's important to keep in mind that the more the lines between personal and professional continue to diminish, the more careful you need to be about what you post on Facebook and elsewhere online. If you're using Facebook for career purposes, then don't post anything—photos, status updates, videos, etc.—that you wouldn't be comfortable with a prospective employer seeing. Even if you're not actively job hunting, be careful anyway. What you post can come back to haunt you in the future.

11 Privacy and Safety Issues

How to *Not* Find a Job Online

There is a lot you will need to do to find a job online, but there are also some things you shouldn't do. Some are related to yourself as a candidate. Others are about prospective employers and making sure that the companies you are applying to are legitimate. It's important to review, as well, what employers can do with the information they find out about you, because what they discover can impact whether they hire you or not.

Protect Your Privacy

In a nutshell, you need to be careful. Be careful about the information you share online, in order to protect your privacy and your identity, and careful about the jobs you apply for. It can be easy to be taken advantage of, by scams that charge you money for nonexistent jobs, by others that try to get you to divulge personal confidential information, and by companies that aren't what they advertise themselves to be.

Anyone who puts any information online needs to take measures to protect themselves and their identity. You need to conduct due diligence and take the time to investigate jobs and companies that you apply to, to make sure they are legitimate. It's your responsibility to protect yourself, because, unfortunately there isn't anyone out there policing fraudulent information on the Internet.

There are some simple measures you can utilize that will help you ensure that your job search is a safe one.

Online Job Searching Do's and Don'ts

- **Do** open a dedicated email account for your job search—keep your personal and professional life separate from your job searching one.

- **Don't** use your work email address.

- **Don't** use company computers or phones.

- **Do** use a different user name and password for job searching. Don't use the same login information you use for your personal accounts.

- **Do** keep a copy of your resume online (Google documents or attached to your web-based email) so you can easily access to apply for jobs.

- **Do** be discreet about the fact that you're job searching if you are currently employed.

- **Do** be careful what information you put online. If you put it on the web, someone will read it. That's guaranteed.

- **Do** make sure your professional profiles on LinkedIn, VisualCV, and other business networking sites are complete.

- **Don't** put anything you wouldn't want an employer to see on Facebook, Twitter, or any other social networking site. Make sure your profiles are private and not viewable by the world.

What Employers Can Find Out About You

Many companies conduct background checks before they tender a job offer. What the company finds can preclude you from getting that offer, so it's important to be aware of what employers can find when they run a background check. In some cases, it's a lot of information. It can include your work history (in detail), your credit history, and your arrest record.

J. Steven Niznik, Owner of EmployeeIssues.com, explains: "It's a misconception that it's illegal for employers to disclose information about former employees during employment background checks. Generally, relevant state laws allow employers to disclose information about former employees, as long as the information is truthful, factual, and limited to employment matters."

Keep in mind that, as Steven mentioned, background check laws vary from state to state, so the rules are different depending on where you live. I get more questions than I can keep track of from people who want to know what an employer can ask and what they can't. I also get lots of questions about how getting fired or getting arrested or having credit issues can impact employment. The answer is that it depends, so if you're not sure, check with your State Labor Department or visit EmployeeIssues.com, or another site with labor-related information.

What employers can check:

- Social security number

- Previous employment—dates, salaries

- Credit history

- Driving records

- Criminal record (depending on state law)

What employers cannot check without your permission:

- School records

- Criminal record (depending on state law)

Something to keep in mind, when filling out job applications, is that it is important to tell the truth. If a company checks your background and you lied, you're not going to get a job offer. If you have already been hired, you could be fired at any point in the future. A dean at a top university resigned after more than twenty-five years on the job after it was discovered that she had misrepresented her background when she first applied. A CEO of a major corporation lost over a million dollars in bonus money when it was revealed that his credentials weren't what he claimed. Other CEOs have lost their jobs for falsifying their resumes as well.

It's not only those in top management who lose their jobs for lying. One of the topics discussed a lot in the About.com Job Searching Forum (http://jobsearch.about.com/forum) is what to do when you've been fired. One person, who had been fired for suspicion of theft, didn't mention his termination when applying for new jobs. He then got fired again by a second employer for not disclosing the first termination.

White lies count too, by the way. When you complete job applications and write your resume, be accurate as to when you left and started your jobs. You can get away with using the month/year, rather than the exact date. However, when your background is checked, your previous employer will be asked your starting and ending dates of employment.

Fudging the dates is lying, and lying about your background can, and probably will, come back to haunt you. I spoke to one person recently who had listed a job as lasting six months longer than it had. He had a job offer in hand from a major Wall Street investment firm, but the offer was contingent upon him passing a background check, which was obviously now a big issue.

Please don't lie. You aren't going to gain anything in the long run. It's better to be honest and possibly not get offered the job than it is to have the job offer withdrawn or to get fired later on.

Privacy Concerns

Why is privacy so important? What's the worst that can happen? This is very sad, but a young woman who applied for a nanny job on Craigslist was murdered. The suspect is believed to have posted a fraudulent ad on Craigslist for a babysitter. I'm sure most of us wouldn't have thought of losing our life as a potential outcome of looking for a job, but it did happen, and it should be a strong warning to be careful when job searching.

Hopefully, this was an isolated incident, but consider the consequences of posting information online that gets into the wrong hands. If you post your address, someone can find out where you live. Posting your phone number can also help people track you down. Providing financial information to the wrong people could ruin your credit.

Identity theft is another concern, and posting information in the wrong places can help thieves steal your identity. The last thing you need is someone getting your credit card information and using your accounts. I've had fraudulent charges on my account, even without having a lot of contact information online, and it can be a pain in the neck to get the charges removed.

Don't Share Confidential Information
- User names/passwords

- Bank account number

- Credit card information

- Date of birth

- Driver's license number

- PayPal account number

- Mother's maiden name

- Social Security number

- Spouse's name

- Children's names

Social Networking Privacy Settings

Check the settings on your networking site profiles. If you are a Myspace or Facebook user and are concerned about who is seeing the personal information that you have online, change your privacy setting so only your friends, or people in certain networks or groups, can see your profiles.

What you post online will be held against you, even if it shouldn't be, and it will be found. In a KARE news story (http://tinyurl.com/22vot3) [origin.kare11.com/news/news_article.aspx?storyid=492170] about students being disciplined after school administration found party photos on Facebook, ACLU Executive Director Charles Samuelson was quoted as saying, "Any kid who thinks what they post on a social networking website is private is an idiot." That's a good summary of what you're doing when you're posting online and thinking nobody will find it.

Adjusting your privacy settings is a step in protecting your profile information. Here's how to change them:

Facebook Privacy Settings:
http://tinyurl.com/23gwmg [jobsearch.about.com/od/onlinecareernet-working/qt/facebookprivacy.htm]

How to Avoid Scams

Don't believe everything you read. Unfortunately, especially when you are looking for jobs working at home, there are as many unscrupulous companies and scams than there are legitimate opportunities.

Legitimate companies pay you, not the other way around. If any company wants to charge you a fee to hire you, or get you started, or process the paperwork, run, don't walk, away from the job.

I remember one case where a job seeker got a very detailed email from an employer about the hiring process. She couldn't remember whether she had actually applied to the company or not (that's why it's smart to keep track of your applications). There was a detailed job description, information on the training program, the salary, and the benefits, and when she would start. The catch was that the "employer" needed her bank account information to get her on the payroll and process her application. That's something no employer would need (setting up direct deposit starts once you have been hired already). Plus, she had never actually spoken to anyone at the company.

I can see why she was almost taken in. There are lots of sophisticated scams out there and it can be hard to tell what's legitimate and what isn't.

Companies can be very sneaky. I know of one employer, as an example, who has about twenty different corporate names. The company describes itself as a high-end advertising/public relations firm and is always seeking recent college graduates who want to start a career in the field. The job actually entails door-to-door sales and multilevel marketing, neither of which is explained in any of the job postings I've seen. It took quite a bit of research to find out what the company actually was doing and how it was misrepresenting itself to applicants.

To be sure, check out the company in advance:

- Better Business Bureau (http://search.bbb.org/searchform.aspx)

- Federal Trade Commission (http://www.ftc.gov)

- Google the company to see what you can find about them online

- Scam.com

Email is another way job seekers can be taken advantage of (it's called *phishing*—a fraudulent attempt at getting confidential information). It happened to a major job site last year when job seeker records were stolen by Trojan horse software. The stolen information included names, addresses, phone numbers, and email addresses. A phishing email was sent to the candidates whose data was stolen, along with a Trojan horse, which looked for bank and credit card account information on their computers.

The job site immediately notified the job seekers and took preventive measures to preclude future problems. If problems can happen on one of the top job sites, imagine the potential for damage if you're posting information all over the Internet.

Monster has excellent advice on email phishing (http://help.monster.com/besafe/email/) you can review to be sure you are job searching safely. Besides protecting yourself from attacks on your computer, don't set yourself up for a problem. You don't need to provide confidential information when you're applying for jobs. At that stage of the hiring process, companies don't need it.

Confidential Job Searching

Confidential job searching is important for a few reasons. First of all, it's a way to protect your privacy. Secondly, if you're employed, it's a way to job search without your current employer finding out that you are in the market for a new job.

There are ways you can job search confidentially online without your boss finding out. Remember that email address just for job searching I mentioned earlier? You should be using that. Again, don't use your work computer or phone to job search. Use your cell phone number. Consider using a generic company name (Online Media Company, for example) instead of the name of your real employer. Remember, most resume databases and networking sites are searchable by company name, so if you make yours anonymous it won't show up in the search results.

If you post your resume online, consider using sites where you can list it confidentially or where you can block some of the information. For example, Monster job seekers can make their resumes confidential and your contact information won't be displayed. You can also block your current employer's name from showing. Yahoo! Hot Jobs and other sites provide similar confidential job seeking services, so check to make sure you can post your resume and apply confidentially for jobs before you upload your resume.

Don't tell the world that you're looking for a job. If you mention it to the person in the next cubicle, that person might just happen to mention it to someone else, and before you know it, your supervisor will know. Definitely don't send an email to your contacts letting them know you're in the market; someone could very easily forward it to your boss.

Tell only those who need to know that you're looking for a job, unless you're out of work, and then you can tell the world. In that case, you'll want all the job search assistance you can get.

RELATED RESOURCES

- Confidential Job Searching (http://tinyurl.com/2p8dcv) [jobsearch.about.com/od/jobsearchhelp/a/ confidentsearch.htm]

- Job Search Internet Privacy (http://tinyurl.com/3cy8r8) [jobsearch.about.com/od/jobsearchprivacy/ Job_Search_Internet_Privacy.htm]

- Monster.com Safe Job Searching (http://help.monster.com/besafe)

---

12 Job Search Tips from the Experts

Many of the leading authorities in the field of employment have shared some of their best job search strategies. These experts in job search and career development techniques were have graciously provided their best tips on how to maximize your potential to land a job in a competitive job market.

The Internet Is Your New Resume

"The Internet is the new resume. That changes everything for the job hunter. Why? Because, in the days before the Internet, you could pretty much control what a prospective employer would know about you. The original resume was distinctive, not only for what it revealed, but also for what it hid. If you had ever been indiscreet, or whatever, but didn't mention that in your resume, it was hard for an employer to find it out, short of hiring a private detective. But now that the Internet is here, it is essentially your new resume, and that changes the whole ball game. You can't, any longer, control what a prospective employer can find out about you. Your Facebook page, photos, tweets, and blogs, are all perused by a prospective employer. And surveys of employers reveal that they frequently turn down a candidate for a job vacancy, based on what they see about him or her on the Internet. You have to pay a lot of attention to what is up there on the Internet about you. Of course, if you know that, you can use the Internet to your advantage, by constantly tweeting, blogging, etc., about things you want the prospective employer to know about you. If the Internet is your new resume, it is also your new press agent and marketing hire."

Dick Bolles, Author, *What Color Is Your Parachute: A Practical Manual for Job-Hunters and Career-Changers*, the most popular job hunting book in the world, with over 10 million copies in print, used in twenty-six countries around the world (http://jobhuntersbible.com)

Use a Personalized Mix of Sites and Strategies

"One key to success in online job searching is to take advantage of the breadth of the web by using a personalized mix of sites, tactics and strategies. Whether it's through social networking, online job sites, blogging or Twitter, job seekers need to choose how they want to balance their search and make it work for them."

Rosemary Haefner, Vice President of Human Resources, Career-Builder (http://careerbuilder.com)

Focus Your Job Search

"Stay focused in your search—on the employers that interest you, the industries that excite you, and the locations that draw you. Limit your search for employment listings to those resources that focus on these same topics, and network with others who share your interests, both online and in person. And always take advantage of the opportunity to meet new people in casual settings that may turn into new professional relationships."

Margaret Riley Dikel, Author, Riley Guide (http://rileyguide.com)

The New Google Theory of Ethics

"Everything you do online now is a representation of the work you will do with your new employer. Everything! From profile images, to links on your LinkedIn account, if it's out there, a hiring manager is making a careful assessment of your candidacy. Take your time and consider what they are looking for in a candidate, and what you can demonstrate which will separate you from everyone else. Remember, qualifications are a commodity; your personality is unique."

Joshua Waldman, Author, Career Enlightenment blog (http://careerenlightenment.net/)

Send a Greeting Card

"Online Job searching has become very impersonal from the job seeker's perspective and the employer's. To stand out from the pack, use a common offline tactic in your job search. Send the employer or recruiter a greeting card after you've sent in your resume, thanking them in advance for reviewing your resume and their consideration. Obviously it's also a good idea to send one after an interview. But what people rarely do is send a thank you card even after being rejected for a job. Many recruiters and employers are impressed by this simple action and will often keep you in mind for another job. A real physical greeting card that was hand written and sent by postal mail can go a long way in a world where shooting off an email is the norm."

Eddy Salomon, Founder, WorkatHomeCareers.com (http://www.workathomecareers.com) and WorkatHomeNoS-cams.com (http://www.workathomenoscams.com)

This Is a Numbers Game

"I have been finding people jobs since 1973 and the most important issue that a person has to remember in looking for a job is to focus on the process of finding a job, rather than the result. Don't worry about getting a job as much as focus on the numbers. This is a numbers game, pure and simple. Numbers of contacts, the numbers of phone calls, numbers of interviews, numbers of follow ups—numbers, numbers, numbers! Now the quality of the "numbers" has to be good, but it begins and ends with numbers. If you focus on the process of the numbers, finding a job will eventually happen."

Tony Beshara, Recruiter; Career Expert; and Author, *The Job Search Solution*

Fit, Fun, and Finance

"Fit, fun, and finance. Find a job or career that combines all three, and you will enjoy every day, and work won't seem like work."

David Culverwell, Cofounder, SuccessHawk (http://www.successhawk.com)

The Biggest Mistakes

"What are the biggest mistakes job seekers make when looking for a job online?

1. Not practicing a safe job search
2. Not following directions implicitly included in the job posting description
3. Not effectively managing your time online
4. Sounding too desperate and sending out mass resumes, emails and cover letters without a strategy or plan in place"

Katrina Kibben, Social Media Ninja, Monster (http://monster.com)

Be Found When Someone Googles You

"In today's job market place, you cannot ignore the power of search and the Internet. Recruiters and potential employers *will* Google you to find out as much as they can about you when making a hiring decision. You have to figure out what your brand is about, and what kind of job you are looking for. Then, go out and find those communities that are already speaking about it, and be heard. Do a Google search for the type of work you are looking for plus the word 'blog' and start commenting on posts of the top five of them. You already have solid proof that those blogs are visible when using Google search. So, be found when someone Googles YOU."

Vickie Smith-Siciuliano, Social Media Consultant, Say WOW Marketing (http://saywowmarketing.com/)

Be Proactive

"I recommend that job seekers be proactive in their job search by reaching out to individuals and companies that may be aware of available jobs in the candidate's specific field of interest. For example, I believe networking is the number one strategy for finding a job. You never know who knows whom, and by reaching out to your personal and professional contacts, you may be pleasantly surprised as to the number of people who are willing and able to help. I recommend joining and searching through social networking sites like Facebook and LinkedIn to find additional ways that you can expand on your overall network. I also recommend that job seekers research companies in desired locations who may also have relevant jobs available. As for the multitude of job search sites out there, I say to review them on a periodic basis but don't make the mistake of making them the only or the focal point of your job search."

Penny Loretto, Career Counselor, Skidmore College
(http://cms.skidmore.edu/career/);
Career Choice (http://www.careerchoic.com/cc/home.php); **and About.com's Guide to Internships** (http://internships.about.com/)

Apply Direct at the Company's Website

"Apply through the hiring company's website. This typically gets you treated as a more serious applicant than someone who applies through a third-party job site. Also, tailor your application to the company and the position. Demonstrate, as specifically as possible, how you can help that company and that hiring manager with their particular needs. Don't just recite your credentials."

Mark Kolakowski, About.com Guide to Financial Careers
(http://financecareers.about.com/)

Kill Trees

"If you apply to a job—or even look at one twice—print it out on a dead tree and keep it in a folder dedicated to your current job search. This helps avoid the embarrassment of applying to the same job twice, lets you recall the details on a job after the company takes it offline, and gives you a fantastic portrait on the kinds of jobs (and especially keywords) that keep triggering your interest. And after you get that new great job, plant a maple!"

Eric Caron, Evangelist, LinkUp (http://www.linkup.com/)

Build a Targeted Job Search Strategy

"Many out there today are pursuing every job that includes the word 'manager' or 'finance' or 'IT.' Because they think: 'You never know when someone might find your background compelling.' But a lack of focus will hurt you. So build a list of target companies. As your networking partner, I need to know that information. Not just that you are looking for 'something stable.' Be able to tell me your specific job search objectives. While you can be open to a lot of job types, I want to know specifics. Specifics will give you a chance to be 'top of mind' with your network. Vague objectives simply leave you in the middle of the stack of business cards I picked up this week."

Tim Tyrell-Smith, Tim's Strategy—Ideas for Job Search Career and Life blog (http://timsstrategy.com)

Don't Spread Yourself Too Thin

"When networking online, don't spread yourself too thin. Choose two to three networking sites and invest your time in actively connecting and participating in those few sites as opposed to being an absentee member of too many networks. Try to invest a few minutes on each site two to three times per week, connecting, responding to messages or discussions, and posting your own messages or starting discussions."

Andrea Santiago, Guide to Health Careers for About.com (http://healthcareers.about.com)

Set Up Google Alerts

"An extremely powerful online job search tool is Google Alerts. Automatically monitor the career pages of your target company's site for new jobs they post, in real time as they occur. As a Java Programmer looking for positions at United Health Group's Minnesota locations you can set up an alert string like: site:careers.unitedhealthgroup.com minnesota java. Most companies post positions on their own site before they are posted on any external job boards, and many positions are never posted externally at all. The notification you will get of the new postings will make you aware of them before most everyone else! You can set up as many alerts as you'd like, for as many companies, and variations of search words as you'd like—be creative!"

Harry Urschel, Owner, e-Executives; and Author, The Wise Job Search blog (http://www.thewisejobsearch.com**)**

Set Up RSS Feeds with Your Job Search Parameters

"Instead of visiting your favorite job sites and search engines every day, set up RSS feeds with your job search parameters. You can do this with Craigslist, Indeed.com, Monster.com, USAJobs.com, and SimplyHired.com, just to name a few. Set up the feed with what you're looking for, such as location and job title, and your feeds will deliver almost instant updates to your RSS reader, saving you a lot of time and energy."

Wendy Boswell, Editor, About.com Web Search (http://websearch.about.com/**); and Author, *The About.com Guide to Online Research***

Be Prepared for Future Job Searches

"As you do your job search, keep in mind that you will likely be in transition in three to five years. I know this sounds bad but if you consider the rest of your career, with multiple job searches (aka, transitions), and you do each job search like it isn't the last one, you'll be much better prepared for future job searches. This will affect your attitude, which will affect your demeanor, which will have an impact on your networking and communications, which can lead you to a job lead faster. This is not a one-time situation; this is a career skill."

Jason Alba, Founder, JibberJobber, (http://jibberjobber.com/); **and Author,** *I'm On LinkedIn—Now What???* (http://imonlinkedinnowwhat.com)

Set Up Automated Reminders

"Don't get bogged down with trolling the Internet for job postings. Set up an automated reminder with a site like Indeed.com, and focus the energy elsewhere such as setting up coffee appointments with old friends and past coworkers or picking up a new hobby. Hours a day wandering the net can be very depressing. Take advantage of the technology available and instead focus on thinking about what you really want to do when you grow up."

Thomas Chambers, Executive Search Recruiter, firstPRO Inc. (http://www.firstproinc.com/aboutus.aspx)

Everyone Needs to Be ABL

"The velocity of job changes continues regardless of any economic recovery. Long-term prospects for job seekers are that everyone will need to be ABL—'always be looking.' People need to be proficient at job seeking or leverage services like JobSerf—or be prepared for numerous painful employment and resume gaps."

Jay Martin, Founder, JobSerf (http://jobserf.com)

A Top Job and Networking Websites

General Job Searching Sites

- About.com Guide to Job Searching (http://jobsearch.about.com)

- Job-Hunt (http://www.job-hunt.org)

- The Riley Guide (http://www.rileyguide.com)

Job Banks

- CareerBuilder.com

- Dice.com

- Monster.com

Job Search Engines

- Indeed.com

- LinkUp.com

- SimplyHired.com

Entry Level Job Sites

- CareerRookie.com

- CollegeGrad.com

- CollegeRecruiter.com

- Experience.com

Seasonal/Part-Time Job Sites

- Coolworks.com

- SnagAJob.com

Local Job Sites

- Craigslist (http://craigslist.org)

- Job-Hunt.org Resources by State
  (http://job-hunt.org/jobs/states.shtml)

- Online Newspapers (http://jobsearch.about.com/od/newspapers)

- State and Local Job Sites
  (http://jobsearch.about.com/od/statejobslist)

Niche Job Sites

- Dice.com (tech jobs)

- Elance.com (freelance jobs)

- EscapeArtist.com (international jobs)

- Healthcareers.about.com (health care jobs)

- Internships.about.com (internships)

- MediaBistro.com (media jobs)

- Net-Temps.com (temporary jobs)

- TransitionsAbroad.com (international jobs)
- USAJobs (http://usajobs.opm.gov) (government jobs)
- Directory of Niche Sites (http://tinyurl.com/2ee2sv) [jobsearch.about.com/od/jobsbycareerfieldaz/a/topsbytype.htm]

Networking Sites
- 85broads.com
- Facebook.com
- LinkedIn.com
- Twitter.com
- MyWorkster.com
- Ning.com
- Ryze.com
- Twitter.com
- Yahoo! KickStart

Company and Occupational Information
- About.com Guide Career Planning (http://careerplanning.about.com)
- Company Research (http://jobsearch.about.com/od/companyresearch)
- Jobstar.org
- Monster Major to Career Converter (http://tinyurl.com/4f6yv9z) [content.monstertrak.monster.com/tools/careerconverter]

- Occupational Outlook Handbook
  (http://stats.bls.gov/oco/home.htm)

- Vault.com

Professional Branding

- CareerDistinction.com

- Personal Branding Blog
  (http://personalbrandingblog.wordpress.com)

Job Search Blogs

- Alison Doyle Blog (http://alisondoyle.typepad.com)

- Another Point of View (http://anotherpointofview.typepad.com)

- Blog Indeed (http://blog.indeed.com)

- CoolWorks Blog (http://www.coolworks.com/blogs)

- JibberJobber Blog (http://jibberjobber.com/blog)

- LinkedIn Blog (http://blog.linkedin.com)

- Monster Blog (http://monster.typepad.com)

- Secrets of the Job Hunt (http://secretsofthejobhunt.com)

- SimplyBlog (http://blog.simplyhired.com)

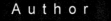

About the Author

Alison Doyle is a job search and employment expert with many years of experience in human resources, career development, and job searching, with a focus on online job searching, job search technology, social media, and professional networking.

Alison has covered job searching (http://jobsearch.about.com) for About.com (a *New York Times* Company) since 1998. She is the author of *Internet Your Way to a New Job* and *The About.com Guide to Job Searching*. More information on Alison's expertise is available on AlisonDoyle.com (http://alisondoyle.com).

Other Happy About® Books

Purchase these books at Happy About http://happyabout.com or at other online and physical bookstores.

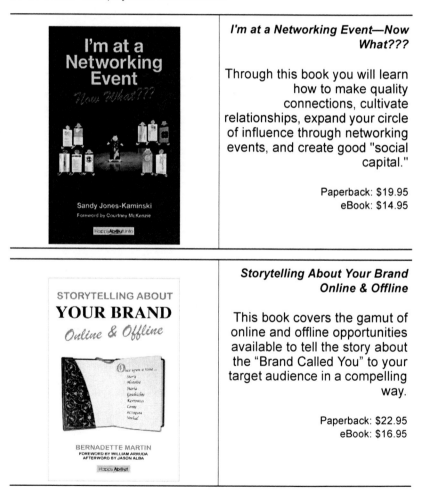

I'm at a Networking Event—Now What???

Through this book you will learn how to make quality connections, cultivate relationships, expand your circle of influence through networking events, and create good "social capital."

Paperback: $19.95
eBook: $14.95

Storytelling About Your Brand Online & Offline

This book covers the gamut of online and offline opportunities available to tell the story about the "Brand Called You" to your target audience in a compelling way.

Paperback: $22.95
eBook: $16.95

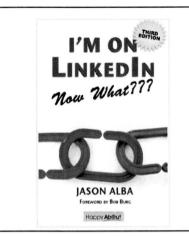

I'm on LinkedIn—Now What???

This book explains the benefits of using LinkedIn and recommends best practices so that you can get the most out of it.

Paperback: $19.95
eBook: $14.95

Happy About My Resume

The average recruiter or hiring manager spends less than 15 seconds reviewing a resume. Most people's resumes fail to "wow" the reader and quickly end up in the "no" pile.

Paperback: $19.95
eBook: $14.95